JOURNEYS INTO BUCKINGHAMSHIRE

A COLLECTION OF
INK DRAWINGS

BY

ANTHONY MACKAY

FOREWORD BY

SIR FRANCIS DASHWOOD, Bt

First published in Great Britain

November 1998

by

The Book Castle

12 Church Street

Dunstable

Bedfordshire

ISBN 1 871199 14 X

Typeset by
Palfrey Advertising and Design
Edlesborough, Buckinghamshire

Printed and bound by
Interprint Ltd.,
Malta

CONTENTS

WEST COMMON, GERRARDS CROSS

Dedicated to
Katie

THE OUSE AT THORNBOROUGH

FOREWORD
by
SIR FRANCIS DASHWOOD, Bt

WEST WYCOMBE PARK

It gives me great pleasure to write this foreword. Anthony Mackay has produced a most delightful collection of ink drawings of the landscape and buildings of Buckinghamshire. These are the result of several years of sketching and historical studies and represent an important record of our environment at the end of the 20th Century.

The drawings show the variety of architecture and the beautiful Chiltern Landscape which is largely unspoilt, in spite of being so close to the heavily populated area of Greater London. Our county offers a wonderful escape for people for a wide range of leisure activities.

This book will surely stimulate interest in the county and will encourage exploration of its many unique facilities.

Francis Dashwood

Sir Francis Dashwood, Bt

ACKNOWLEDGEMENTS

For permission to make drawings and to use them in this volume, I would like to thank the following individuals and institutions, who kindly allowed me onto their land and gave me invaluable help in compiling information about their buildings:

Annie, Rose Cottage, Adstock
Bletchley Park Trust, Bletchley Park, Bletchley
The late Mrs P Brunner, Wotton House, Wotton Underwood
Buckinghamshire County Council, Aylesbury
Mr and Mrs Nigel Budden, High and Over, Amersham
Mr Barry Clayton, Tyringham Gatehouse, Tyringham
Mr Geoffrey Clements, Maharishi Foundation, Mentmore House
The Hotel Manager, Cliveden House
Mrs Danny, Notley Abbey, Long Crendon
Sir Francis Dashwood, West Wycombe House, West Wycombe
Mrs Pippa Deacon, Old Manor House, Thornborough
The Friends Meeting House, Jordans
Gayhurst Court Management Company, Gayhurst
Mrs Griffin, Keeper of the Collection, Waddesdon Manor, Waddesdon
The Hotel Manager, Hartwell House, Hartwell

Mr and Mrs Howarth, Radclive Manor, Radclive
Mr Philip King, (NT Custodian), Claydon House
Mr Andrew Kingsmill, Salden House, Mursley
Jonathan and Medina Marks, Tythrop House, Kingsey
Paddy and Jette McCowan, Old Farmhouse, Little Horwood
Milton Museum Curator, Milton's Cottage, Chalfont St Giles
The National Trust, Cliveden, Waddesdon and Stowe
Mr and Mrs Neill, The Homestead, Worminghall
Peregrine and Jill Palmer, Dorney Court, Dorney
Mr Frank Thompson, (NT Custodian), Stowe
Mr P J Welsh, Managing Director Tyringham Clinic
Mr and Mrs W G Williams, Shakespeare House, Grendon Underwood
Mrs V Willis, Swanbourne House School
Doctors Pridie, Long Crendon Manor
Mr Robert Spencer Bernard, Nether Winchendon House

For her invaluable support during the last three years of work, I particularly wish to thank my wife Elaine.

For countless refreshment stops may I thank all at Carrington's Cafe in Old Amersham.

ROSE COTTAGE, ADSTOCK

INTRODUCTION

BEECHES AT WHITELEAF

Buckinghamshire is almost entirely rural, straddling the Chilterns, the Vale of Aylesbury and the Great Ouse Valley, brushing the banks of the Thames in the south and the borders of Northamptonshire in the north. It is flanked by Oxfordshire to the west and by Bedfordshire and Hertfordshire to the east.

Although physically unspectacular, there are places where the chalk escarpment rises sharply, opening up panoramic views over wide expanses of green farmland and where river valleys are as pastoral and peaceful as any countryside in England.

Broadly speaking, it is a land of subtle contrasts and close harmonies demanding detailed study. Cycling the lanes and walking the extensive footpath network bring you into intimate contact with an agricultural landscape crafted and honed by man and the elements over many centuries.

Proximity to London has had a major influence on the buildings of the county. Eminent families have built stately homes and created magnificent parks and, in the absence of major cities, there is a scattering of substantial market towns of medieval structure. The great attraction of Buckinghamshire lies in its ancient villages with their exquisite parish churches and richly varied domestic architecture.

The geology of the county is crucial to its character. It is crossed by bands of clay, sand and limestone running broadly in a south westerly to north easterly direction, creating great natural variety both in the flora and fauna and in the building materials used. The Chilterns stretch right across the county and, although the chalk itself is not a significant source of building material, the flints allied to it have been extensively used in combination with brick dressings. Local building stone is scarce in Buckinghamshire but Cotswold limestone and Northamptonshire ironstone quarries have proved convenient sources. However, in the Ouse Valley, the town of Olney and several neighbouring villages, including Newton Blossomville and Weston Underwood, not to mention the magnificent mansion at Stowe, were built almost entirely of locally quarried limestone. Most parish churches in the northern half of the county were built of Purbeck and Portland limestone. With the coming of brick manufacture to the region during the 16th and 17th centuries, stone was superceded as the dominant building material. There are many surviving examples of timber-framed construction, usually in conjunction with wattle and daub or brick infill walls and thatch was the most common roofing material until clay tiles took over. In the western part of the Vale of Aylesbury in and around Haddenham, witchert was a traditional form of walling construction.

The pre-history of Buckinghamshire throws up few significant monuments, although Ice Age tools have been recovered from soft river valley deposits and from the Chilterns. Once the ice had retreated, substantial forest colonised the land and man, who was then becoming more sedentary and developing agricultural methods, was forced to make clearances in which to grow cereal crops.

The round barrow at Whiteleaf Hill near Princes Risborough dates from about 3500 BC. The Neolithic and Early Bronze Ages bequeathed flint axes and arrowheads and, at Bledlow and Ravenstone, are surviving barrows from these periods. Iron Age hillforts are situated long the ridge at Ivinghoe Beacon, Cholesbury and Great Kimble and parts of Grim's Ditch appear in places, between Bradenham and Wendover.

The Roman Occupation brought significant changes to the infrastructure with the building of Watling Street and Akeman Street. Several important sites have been excavated at Magiovinium (Bow Brickhill), Bancroft (Milton Keynes), Hambledon, Chenies and Tingewick. During the Anglo-Saxon period, the countryside was cleared of much of its forest and became predominantly agricultural, giving rise to important market centres like Buckingham, Newport Pagnell, Aylesbury and High Wycombe. Little of the architecture of the period survives, although substantial late Saxon churches at Wing and Lavendon are remarkable exceptions.

Norman churches are plentiful with leading examples at Stewkley and Shenley Church End and many fine decorative doorways and tympana are to be found across the county.

The main period of church building was from the 14th to the 16th century with fine Decorated work at Olney, Great Horwood and Great Missenden and the best of the Perpendicular style at Cublington, Hillesden, Maids' Morton and High Wycombe.

The only castle remains are earth mounds of motte and bailey structures, notably at Castlethorpe and Whitchurch, but moats are plentiful, with good examples at Boarstall and Quainton. There were royal palaces at Brill, where King Edward the Confessor maintained a hunting lodge until 1337 and at Princes Risborough, where the Black Prince had a manor.

The remains of medieval domestic buildings are rare, but fragments exist at Sycamore Farm in Long Crendon, at Denham Court, Creslow Manor and Dorney Court. The King's Head in Aylesbury is a magnificently preserved 15th century inn. After the Dissolution of the Monasteries during the 1530s, many religious houses, including Notley Abbey and Chenies, were converted to domestic use.

The 17th and 18th centuries saw major changes in house design with the extensive use of brick with stone dressings, hipped roofs and cross-mullioned windows. The manors at Princes Risborough and Bradenham, Tythrop House at Kingsey and Winslow Hall by Wren, illustrate this shift in style and materials. Other developments using giant pilasters, pediments and parapets can be seen at Wotton Underwood, Chicheley and Iver Grove. Public buildings also showed similar changes with the building of the Palladian style Guildhall at High Wycombe and the Baroque County Hall at Aylesbury. Major houses at Oving, Shardeloes, Claydon and Harleyford continued this movement into the late 18th century, culminating in Adam's masterpiece at Stowe and the Dashwoods' house at West Wycombe.

SHAKESPEARE HOUSE, GRENDON UNDERWOOD

BURNHAM COTTAGE, LONG CRENDON

Ecclesiastical buildings of this period include Robert Hooke's minor masterpiece, Willen church in Milton Keynes, the church at Gayhurst, Palladian West Wycombe church and the Gothic church at Hartwell. Non-Conformist chapels sprang up in converted barns or cottages. The Friends' Meeting House at Jordans was purpose-built in 1668, immediately after the Toleration Act, and prominent meeting houses followed at Aylesbury, Chesham, Winslow and Amersham.

The Victorian period saw an explosion in church building, led by the powerful designs of Street and George Gilbert Scott, with classic examples of the Gothic style at Coleshill, Fenny Stratford and Dropmore.

Remarkably lavish country houses were built during this period, by the Rothschilds at Waddesdon, Mentmore and Ascott and by the Astors at Cliveden. Other notable major houses, either built or adapted at the time, include Hughenden, Danesfield and Taplow Court. In parallel with the growth of church and country house building, there was significant development in the industrial field. Earlier domestic industries, like lace-making and straw plaiting, died out in the early 19th century and furniture-making in the High Wycombe area became mechanised. However, paper-making and printing, brewing, milling and brick-making continued throughout the period. Bletchley and Wolverton became important railway towns and the eastern parts of the county were connected by the Grand Union Canal, with branches constructed to Wendover, Buckingham, Aylesbury and Newport Pagnell. Major engineering projects symbolised the revolution in industry. At Old Wolverton, the Iron Trunk was built in 1809-11 to carry the canal over the Ouse and the fourth oldest cast-iron bridge was built at Newport Pagnell. In 1829-31 a wrought iron suspension bridge was constructed over the Thames at Marlow and, at Taplow, Brunel built the beautiful Maidenhead railway bridge on the Great Western Line.

During the early 20th century new settlements grew up around stations at Amersham, Beaconsfield, Chesham, Great Missenden, Wendover, Marlow and the Chalfonts, and South Buckinghamshire rapidly became a rural suburbia. In the second half of the century public building has focussed on county council schools and the creation of Milton Keynes, the rationalised traditional style of the former contrasting sharply with the more radical approach of the latter.

Amongst the most enduring images I have of Buckinghamshire are towering beechwoods pierced by shafts of dazzling sunlight, ravishing views across the Vale of Aylesbury, the tranquillity of the Ouse as it slides through fields near Newport Pagnell and evening light on tree-clad hills at the heart of the Chilterns.

I enjoy the market town elegance of Old Amersham, the busy little square at Winslow and the lively High Street of Stony Stratford. Ageing Dorney Court, where the same family has been in residence since the 16th century, has a unique atmosphere. The impressive 14th century structure of Thornborough bridge, the Saxon church at Wing and the decorative masterpiece of Stewkley church are all powerful statements. High on my list are the harmonious two-storeyed colonnade on the south front of West Wycombe House, the curious mixture of architectural styles which make up Nether Winchendon House and majestic Cliveden, perched on its airy elevated site, overlooking a leafy and sinuous stretch of the Thames. A memorable place is Old Farmhouse at Little Horwood, little altered since the 16th century and a perfect combination of timber framing, thatch and mellow brickwork, set in an exquisite terraced garden. Finally, I should mention romantic Notley Abbey, nestling in a sublime valley and embodying so much of the medieval period.

Most of these places are rooted in the past, but the brave 1930s houses at Amersham and Dagnall and the gravel pits at Willen, transformed into sparkling lakes teeming with wildlife, demonstrate that our own times have also made a lasting contribution.

DINTON CHURCH AND GREEN

WHADDON CHURCH

x

This brief introduction has somewhat skimmed over the history and the development of the county, but the topics and places mentioned are dealt with in fuller detail under the individual chapter entries. My illustrations represent a highly personal choice and it is hoped that the historical notes provide a fitting balance. Ideally, the drawings alone should speak for me and encourage readers to make their own personal journeys into this largely unsung part of rural England.

Anthony Mackay
Bedford 1998

ILMER CHURCH

MAP OF BUCKINGHAMSHIRE

THE OUSE VALLEY, MILTON KEYNES AND BUCKINGHAM

The Great Ouse rises just over the county boundary in Northamptonshire, wriggles almost imperceptibly down to Buckingham and, fed by countless streams, widens to become a substantial river by the time it reaches Milton Keynes and Newport Pagnell, warranting sturdy stone bridges and controlling weirs. It then meanders majestically northwards and eastwards through Olney and crosses into Bedfordshire on its long journey to the North Sea.

The river dominates the northern part of the county, dictating the form of settlements and shaping the engineering structures which enable roads and railways to pass through. Frequent flooding of the river plain has constrained urban development and allowed a predominantly pastoral landscape of water meadows fringed by gentle slopes of agricultural and grazing land.

The once-great Whittlewood and Salcey forests have left tiny woodland remnants in Buckinghamshire near Stowe and Stoke Goldington and, although the landscape boasts many splendid trees and mature hedgerows, the overall impression is of open undulating farmland. Only at the Brickhills ridge does the land rise steeply into dense forest.

The town of Olney is the focus of the most northerly part of the county, its long market street lined with elegant stone houses and culminating in a landmark church spire on the banks of the Ouse. Most of the surrounding villages are built of local stone and there are fine country houses at Chicheley, Tyringham and Gayhurst. The M1 motorway cuts a swathe through the county close to Newport Pagnell, which retains its historic character despite recent growth.

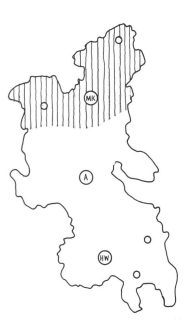

RUSHMERE COTTAGE, GREAT HORWOOD

During the last three decades of the twentieth century the city of Milton Keynes has transformed a large part of North Buckinghamshire. Existing ancient coaching towns on Watling Street and the railway towns of Bletchley and Wolverton, through a radical town planning concept, have been incorporated into a new garden-city of low-rise buildings immersed in an enveloping carpet of trees and planted parkways. The landscape is further enriched by a string of wildlife and recreational lakes fashioned out of former industrial gravel pits.

To the west is Buckingham, a quiet market town cresting a low hill in a loop of the River Ouse. Nearby, the magnificent former home of the Temple-Grenville family at Stowe is now a public school and the park, with its temples, lodges and statuary, is managed by the National Trust.

The landscape is sprinkled with small villages built in stone and timber-framing, the most picturesque of which are Padbury, the Lillingstones and the Horwoods. The small town of Winslow signals a distinct shift to brick as the main building material, with its captivating houses and the imposing Winslow Hall by Wren.

Winding through the eastern part of this region from Wolverton to Soulbury, en route from the Midlands to London, the Grand Union Canal makes a significant impact on the landscape with its historic Iron Trunk section over the Ouse at Wolverton, singular brick bridges, colourful barges and clusters of captivating locks.

THE OUSE AT OLNEY

2

OLNEY

Formerly a lace-making centre, the town is distinguished by its long main street, which widens at the southern end to form the market place and by the lofty spire of the 14th century church, which dominates the Ouse valley for miles around. Beautifully detailed limestone houses, narrow alleyways to rear courtyards and many antique furniture shops, characterise this busy town, which has become nationally renowned for the Pancake Race held each Shrove Tuesday and dating back to 1445.

William Cowper, the poet, lived for nineteen years, from 1767, in a house on the market square, which is now a museum devoted to the life and works of Cowper and of John Newton, a former curate of the church, who composed the Olney hymns, including 'Amazing Grace' and 'How sweet the name of Jesus sounds', and was a colleague of William Wilberforce, the anti-slave-trade campaigner.

OLNEY CHURCH AND MILL HOUSE

HIGH STREET, OLNEY

4

WESTON UNDERWOOD; RAVENSTONE; STOKE GOLDINGTON; HANSLOPE

Weston House at *Weston Underwood* was the home of the Throckmorton family which angered Queen Elizabeth I by its championing of Mary, Queen of Scots, and several members were imprisoned in the Tower or hanged at Tyburn. The only remains of the house are an early 18th century wing, part of the chapel and the former stables, clock house and gatepiers on the village High Street.

The poet, Cowper, a friend of the Throckmortons, moved from Olney to Weston Underwood in 1786 and lived in the lodge until 1795.

St Laurence Church has 13th century arcades and perpendicular windows. Features include box pews and several 14th century stained glass figures in the east window.

At *Ravenstone*, a long village street of thatched ironstone cottages rises to the church of All Saints, a Norman building with 13th century tower and later additions by Heneage Finch, Lord Chancellor to King Charles II.

There are some traces of Ravenstone Augustinian Priory nearby. The Finch Almshouses, built in the late 17th century, comprise two facing rows of single-storey chequered brick buildings.

The straggly village of *Stoke Goldington* has many good stone cottages and farm buildings, but is assaulted by heavy through traffic.

St Peter's Church has a Norman chancel arch and 13th century arcades.

Church Farmhouse is late 16th century.

The 180 foot high spire of St James's Church, *Hanslope*, is a prominent landmark. The chancel is late Norman and the aisles were added in the 13th century.

On The Green stands Old Manor House Farm, a 17th century stone house with 18th century brick additions, mullioned windows and massive stone chimney stacks with brick shafts.

COWPERS LODGE, WESTON UNDERWOOD

Other fine 17th century buildings in the village include Maltings Farmhouse (1624), Pindon Farmhouse (1656) and Tathall End Farmhouse (1625), with its dovecote dated 1601.

At Bullington End lies Hanslope Park House, a plain stone-faced late 17th century building, the grounds of which were landscaped by Humphrey Repton.

GAYHURST; TYRINGHAM

After the estate park of *Gayhurst* was created in 1737, the village houses and inn were moved on to the main road and the house, stables and church now form an isolated and elegant group approached through parkland laid out by both Capability Brown and Repton.

Gayhurst House was begun in 1597 and is a three storey stone E-plan building with projecting bays. It has mullioned and transomed windows of six or four lights, a porch with two orders of columns and the recessed centre part has five shaped gables with ogee curves and finials The interior was extensively remodelled during the 18th century, affecting ceilings. fireplaces and staircase William Burges later altered the Abbess's Room, the Dining Room and the Guard Room, and added the Brewhouse, Bakehouse and the Male Servants Lavatory, an extraordinary little building of 1859-60 ressembling the Abbot's Kitchen at Glastonbury. The Gate Lodge is mock Elizabethan and is now the Sir Francis Drake pub, a reference to the fact that the manor of Gayhurst had been given to Sir Francis by Queen Elizabeth on his return from the Indies, before the present house was built.

The Baroque church of St Peter was built in 1728 and stands close to the house.

Tyringham House, bridge, stables and gateway were designed between 1792 and 1799 by Sir John Soane for Sir William Praed, chairman of the Grand Junction Canal Company. It was Soane's first important commission and, although the house has been severely altered by Edwardian additions, the original power of the architect's concept can be seen in the other elements. The gatehouse in particular is a fine composition and was lovingly and sensitively restored in 1977 by architect Barry Clayton, who lives in it.

The River Great Ouse flows majestically through the park, under the bridge and past the church of St Peter, which dates mainly from 1871, but has a 12th century tower arch and a Perpendicular belfry stage.

GAYHURST HOUSE

TYRINGHAM HOUSE ▷

NEWTON BLOSSOMVILLE CHURCH

NORTH CRAWLEY;
CLIFTON REYNES;
NEWTON BLOSSOMVILLE

St Firmin Church, *North Crawley*, has a five bay arcade of 1200 and the only complete painted 15th century screen in the county.

Old Rectory (1799 to 1800), in the High Street, has five bays with a full-height bow in the centre and a Doric doorcase.

Church Farmhouse, in Chequers Lane, is 16th to 17th century and has some close-studded timber-framing and a jettied gable to the north wing.

At East End stands Quakers Farm, a 17th century timber-framed structure with an 18th century brick casing, a panelled Friends Meeting Room and a stone coat-of-arms from Crawley Grange in an outbuilding.

The most delightful building in the village lies towards Chicheley and is a late 16th century timber-framed farm, built on a stone plinth placed within a moat. Old Moat Farm has a jettied north-east front and is two-storeyed on a hall and cross-wing plan.

Clifton Reynes is a good place from which to walk across the Ouse Valley to Olney. The small and intimate Robin Hood Inn lies at the heart of the village.

The medieval Reynes family hall is no more but the family monuments are all in the church of St Mary, including two effigies in black oak dated 1300, a 14th century tomb chest and some late 15th century brasses. The church is embattled, has a Norman tower and a 14th century octagonal font.

The church of St Nicholas in rustic *Newton Blossomville* was built in the early 14th century and stands close to the River Ouse, from where a long village street of stone houses stretches up to the former Manor House (1588).

LAVENDON; EMBERTON; SHERINGTON; CHICHELEY

The Anglo-Saxon tower of St Michael's Church. *Lavendon*, is tall and unbuttressed. Other substantial Saxon remains can be seen in the nave walling and in the chancel. The arcades are 12th and 13th century with circular piers, square abaci and unmoulded pointed arches.

North of the village are the earthwork remains of Lavendon Castle, dating from 1192. Emberton's All Saints Church is a fine Decorated style building with flowing window tracery, especially in the five light east window.

St Laud's Church, *Sherington*, has a 13th century central tower with unusual four-centred relieving arches high up in the Perpendicular top stage.

Sherington Place in Church End is an 18th century house with a dressed limestone facade. Other noteworthy buildings include The Old Rectory in School Lane dated 1607, the village shop, designed as the Parish School by George Gilbert Scott in 1871 and a stone barn, dated 1774, with a traceried window in the north gable..

Chicheley Hall is the focus of this small village and was built by Sir John Chester between 1719 and 1724. The red brick house has giant stone pilasters and dressings and is characterised by many Italian Baroque details. It is possible that Thomas Archer was involved with the design. The entrance hall is panelled and has a classical ceiling panel painted by Kent between 1717 and 1720. The main rooms are on the east front and are handsomely panelled. The principal Drawing Room, or Great Parlour, has Palladian characteristics with door pediments and a bold cornice.

Corinthian pilasters flank the fireplaces both here and in the Gentlemen's Drawing Room. The 18th century Dovecote has an ogee roof and an arcaded timber cupola.

LAVENDON CHURCH

CHICHELEY HALL

10

CASTLETHORPE; HAVERSHAM; LATHBURY

St Simon and St Jude Church, *Castlethorpe*, has a very mixed structure ranging from the north arcade of 1200, to the tower, which was rebuilt in 1729 after a collapse.

Next to the church the motte and bailey castle remains are well-preserved and the site was used as a fortified manor by the Tyrrils, one of whom has a substantial monument in the church dated 1671.

Castle House is a late 16th century stone farmhouse with a large chimneystack.

Manor Farmhouse is 17th century. There is a 15th century stone house in School Lane with two surviving cruck trusses, a solar wing and an upstairs fireplace dated 1661.

Other good buildings are Castlethorpe Lodge (17th century) and Castlethorpe Mill on the River Tove (1671), with much of its machinery in situ.

Haversham's St Mary's Church has evidence in the tower of Norman beginnings but is mainly Decorated and Perpendicular in style.

The Manor lay south of the church within the well-preserved moated site and had a licence to crenellate granted in 1304. A square dovecote dated 1665 has walls lined with stone nest boxes.

Haversham Grange is on the High Street and was a grange of Lavendon Abbey. It has a 14th century hall and a roof of crucks on stone walls. The cross-wing was rebuilt in 1628.

Lathbury Church is a small 12th century building with a fragment of a Norman tympanum, dated 1090-1100, reset in the nave, depicting two beasts and the Tree of Life, a south doorway of 1200 with two orders and a 12th century window over the south arcade. The Decorated chancel has sedilia with ogee cusping, a double piscina and a south window with a circular wheel motif.

Other buildings of note in the village include Lathbury Park of 1801, The Old Rectory (17th century) and Inn Farm, a coaching inn built by the Cubitts in 1830.

CASTLE MOUND AND CHURCH, CASTLETHORPE

NEWPORT PAGNELL

This is a thriving small town close to the M1 motorway which has been greatly boosted by the nearby presence of Milton Keynes. It has a clutch of notable buildings including the church of St Peter and St Paul, a largely 14th century structure with a fine Decorated north porch and a broad pinnacled west tower overlooking the river meadows below. In the High Street stands The Swan Revived with its highly decorative front and fine Jacobean staircase. Over the River Ouzel arches the Tickford Bridge, a beautiful pre-Victorian structure and the oldest iron bridge in England still in use. Several fine brick houses stand in Union Street and Mill Street dating from the 17th to the 19th centuries and, close to the North Bridge, stands a beautiful seven-bay house with parapet and giant pilasters. In Silver Street is Lovat Bank, a grand house built in 1877 for the Taylor family, the mustard manufacturers. It has moulded brick details, large chimneystacks, half-timbering and a corner tourelle. In Pagg's Court is Christie's School House, which was built as a poorhouse in 1702. Next to Tickford Bridge stands Queen Anne's Hospital of 1892 with a row of brick almshouses and a half-timbered warden's house, which is on the site of St John's Hospital, founded in 1287.

ST PETER AND ST PAUL CHURCH ACROSS THE OUZEL

THE COCK AND THE BULL

STONY STRATFORD

Although part of Milton Keynes City, *Stony Stratford* is an old settlement dating back to before the Roman occupation of Britain. Sited where Watling Street crosses the River Great Ouse, it was a focus for travellers and, in 1194, the market was founded. There were many medieval inns along the High Street but it was in the mid-17th century, when the town became the first stop on the coaching route out of London, that several more splendid inns were built. A string of fires during the 18th century meant that most of the timber-framed and thatched dwellings of the town were replaced by stone and brick structures.

The town is remarkable for the length and stylishness of its High Street and noted for its two famous coaching inns, from which the saying, 'cock and bull stories', originates. The Cock Hotel of 1742 is a brick, seven-bay building and the most splendid in town. Next door, and separated by a carriageway, is The Bull Hotel of 1800. Both have enormous old inn signs bracketed over the street.

St Mary and St Giles Church was rebuilt in 1746 following the fire of 1742, incorporating the surviving medieval tower. The tower of St Mary Magdalene also survived the same fire and stands alone down a side passage alongside Tower House.

Horsefair Green is an attractive linear green space lined with trees and flanked by simple Georgian houses. The Old George is 17th century with attractive bays and a well-preserved rear court.

Cofferidge Close and Magdalen Close are sympathetic recent additions to this delightful historic town.

MILTON KEYNES

The new city of *Milton Keynes*, since it was planned in the late 1960s, has outgrown every other settlement in the county. Whereas traditional towns have organic radial plans focussed on a recognisably dense central district, Milton Keynes is based on a network of grid roads designed to spread traffic loads and to disperse the functions of the city across a low density framework. For many this utopian concept is confusing at first and, in its interpretation, the idea has certainly produced a degree of anonymity across the city, which suffers from a clear set of recognisable landmarks by which to orientate one's movements. The idealistic and imaginative concept was devised by Llewellyn-Davies, Weekes, Forestier-Walker and Bor and subsequently realised by a team of architects, engineers and landscape architects working for the Development Corporation. first set up in 1967.

Almost three decades on from those heady beginnings it is possible to measure how the reality on the ground matches up to the ideals.

It is clear that inhabitants rely heavily on car ownership for movements about the city, as the public transport system falls far short of the original intentions. The physical size of the city means that journeys are lengthy and expensive. However the grid road network does seem to have eliminated the congestion which characterises traditional radial plans, and offers a flexible and very attractive system of planted parkways, which effectively by-pass the residential areas. Within the grid squares, which average about one kilometre square, communities have developed with clear individual identities. All grid squares are interlinked by a web of 'Redways', or footpath/ cycleways, which connect under or over the grid roads.

At the centre of the city as a whole, is Central Milton Keynes, which contains the major public buildings and a vast indoor shopping centre, serving not just the city, but a whole region.

The buildings of the city are not the most successful aspect of its development. The imaginative and creative landscaping has transformed an unremarkable tract of north Buckinghamshire with a sumptuous cloak of woodlands, avenues, magnificent parks and glittering lakes. This is the legacy which future generations will appreciate above all.

St Mary Magdalene Church, *Willen*, was designed by Robert Hooke in 1678 and stands on a low hill, overlooking a lake created from disused gravel pits. It is approached from the west along an avenue of limes, is built of red brick with stone dressings and has a richly plastered interior.

St Mary's Church, *Shenley Church End*, has a chancel dating from the end of the l2th century. The 13th century sedilia has two seats with a single arch spanning both.

The redundant church of St Lawrence, *Broughton*, is famous for its wall paintings depicting St George and the Dragon, St Helen and a bishop saint, with the Virgin sheltering souls under her cloak and, on the east wall, a Pieta (1410) with a mutilated Christ surrounded by men holding his heart, bones and other body parts.

Great Linford Church has a 12th century nave and is otherwise of the 13th and 14th centuries.

The Manor House (1720-40) stands in its own park at the north end of the High Street and has a fine Georgian five-bay, two and a half storey stone facade over the earlier 1688 house.

The village of *Old Wolverton* has disappeared but the church remains isolated in a field close to the Grand Union Canal.

Just to the north of the early 19th century Galleon Inn, is the famous Iron Trunk Aqueduct, built between 1809 and 1811, carrying the Grand Union Canal over the River Ouse. The water runs in a square iron-plated trough in two spans, supported centrally on a stone pier

Bletchley is an industrial town, developed in the 19th century around the railway which arrived in 1838, although it does have a medieval village centre slightly removed from the later commercial centre.

St Mary's Church has a Norman south doorway arch, a 13th century chancel and a 14th century south aisle. The 15th century roof has

BLETCHLEY PARK

arch-braces resting on heads There is an alabaster monument to Lord Grey of Wilton who died in 1442 and was the principal landowner in this area.

Bletchley Park in Wilton Avenue was built in 1860 and extended in 1883 for Herbert Leon, a financier and Member of Parliament but became famous as the government intelligence centre during the Second World War, where the Colossus digital computer was developed and where the Nazi Enigma codes were cracked.

THE MANOR HOUSE, GREAT LINFORD

WILLEN CHURCH

LECKHAMPSTEAD; LILLINGSTONE LOVELL; LILLINGSTONE DAYRELL;

The straggly village of *Leckhampstead* has four ends. The church has Norman elements including a beautiful tympanum over the south door with intertwined dragons and a demon. North and south doorways date from 1150 to 1180 and have zigzags on shafts and hoodmoulds.

Lillingstone Lovell crowns a hill where the Church of Assumption forms the focal point. The 13th century tower has a saddleback roof and several good 15th to 16th century brasses.

The former rectory is now called Glebe House (18th century) and stands next to the church. Thatched 18th century stone barns front the road.

St Nicholas, 'The Church in the Fields', at *Lillingstone Dayrell*, has 11th century remnants in the chancel and the tower, but the remainder is mainly of the 13th century with lancets and a splendid east window, dated 1280. The nave arcades are of the early 13th century with three bays of octagonal piers and double-chamfered arches.

There is a beautiful tomb of Paul Dayrell and his wife, dated 1571, and several earlier brasses. The tomb is free-standing in the middle of the chancel and has recumbent effigies on the tomb lid.

Old Tile House (1690s) stands apart in once sumptuous parkland, has a gabled central bay like a porch and a stone doorcase with the arms of Sir Marmaduke Dayrell.

LILLINGSTONE LOVELL

MAIDS' MORTON;
TURWESTON; WESTBURY

The church of St Edmund, *Maids' Morton*, was reputedly built during the 18th century by two maiden sisters, the Peovers of Toddington Manor and is an impressive building, with a sculptural tower of lancets and V-shaped buttresses. The interior is painted white and the window mullions continue down to the floor like a blind screen. The chancel has three blind recesses with triangular heads and the elaborate sedilia have vaulted canopies.

Turweston church has Norman details in the arcade and much 13th to 14th century work, but was largely rebuilt in 1863. The nave has an early 16th century tie-beam roof.

Other buildings of note are Turweston House (mid-Georgian), and Turweston Manor (1630).

St Augustine's Church, *Westbury*, has a late 13th century chancel and 14th century arcades and was restored in 1863 by Street, who designed the saddleback roof on the tower.

HOLLY COTTAGE, MAIDS' MORTON

LAKE PAVILION, STOWE

STOWE

The 18th century mansion and park at *Stowe* form the finest architectural and landscape composition in the county. Built for the Temple-Grenvilles, the house is an enlargement of an earlier house of 1676 for Sir Richard Temple.

The park was designed by William Kent in the 1730s and the head gardener at the time was Lancelot Brown, who later became known as 'Capability'. Stowe is regarded as the birthplace of the quintessentially English art of landscape gardening which spread its influence throughout Europe and beyond.

In 1749 Earl Temple commissioned Robert Adam to design the new south front to the mansion and, subsequently, employed architects Borra and Blondel from Italy and France and the Italian scene-painter Valrati.

Since 1923 Stowe has been a school and, in 1989, the National Trust assumed responsibility for the restoration and maintenance of all those buildings in the grounds which were of no practical use to the school. That process is in the capable hands of architects Inskip and Jenkins.

The South Front is the tour de force of the design and faces the park overlooking lakes across sweeping grassy slopes defined by informally curving stands of mature trees. Amongst the trees and facing the house across the lakes, are pavilions and temples of both classical and Gothic styles.

The house is planned with all the main rooms on the piano nobile. A central block has low wings to either side and higher end pavilions. The eliptical Marble Saloon is flanked by the State Drawing Room and the State Music Room and entered directly from the North Hall. The State Dining Room is in the west wing and the Library in the east wing.

On the ground floor below this level is the Gothic Library designed by Soane in 1805.

The principal buildings in the park are The Temple of Ancient Virtue, the Doric Arch, the Palladian Bridge, the Lake Pavilions. the Temple of British Worthies, the Gothic Temple and the Temple of Concord.

◁ *THE SOUTH FRONT, STOWE*

THE PALLADIAN BRIDGE, STOWE

BOYCOTT PAVILION, STOWE

WATER STRATFORD;
RADCLIVE; TINGEWICK

St Giles' Church, *Water Stratford*, has some outstanding Norman sculpture in the tympani of the north and south doorways.

Radclive nestles beguilingly in a hollow within a loop of the River Great Ouse.

The church of St John the Evangelist is largely of the 13th century but has Norman traces in the arch mouldings and jamb motifs.

The Manor House is 16th century with a timber frame and brick infilling and was enlarged and cased in stone in the early 17th century. There are wooden mullioned and transomed windows and a fine staircase with a balustrade of openwork panels of finial-spike ovals and lozenges. The stone dovecote is 18th century.

The four-arch brick bridge over the river is early 18th century.

Tingewick is unfortunately beset by the noise and pollution of through traffic but has a fine medieval church with a 12th century north aisle and north arcade and a Perpendicular tower. Tingewick Mill(18th century) and the mill house stand together by the Ouse. East of the mill is a Roman Vllla site of the 4th century AD.

Manor Farmhouse is 17th century with one 15th century mullioned window installed.

RADCLIVE BRIDGE

BUCKINGHAM

Although nominally the county town, *Buckingham* has always been somewhat isolated and was rivalled as early as 1218 by Aylesbury, which subsequently became the seat of administration, commerce and the assizes. Today it has neither railway nor motorway connections and still has the character of a pre-Victorian town, making it an attractive place to live and retaining many of its older central buildings.

The town centre stands on a low hill within a loop of the River Ouse. Founded in the 10th century by Edward the Elder as a burh, it probably had Saxon precedents.

The medieval church has gone however and a new church, with a prominent spire, was erected on Castle Hill in the 18th century. The castle itself has also disappeared. The focus of the town was the market place and the town's prosperity was in the wool and cloth trades, which declined during the 15th century. A disastrous fire in 1725 destroyed about a third of the dwellings, although many were rebuilt immediately afterwards.

The Town Hall at the head of the market square was first built in 1685, demolished in 1783 and rebuilt in 1784. It is of brick with a hipped roof and a cupola and an open, arcaded market floor, since enclosed with windows. The gilded copper weather-vane finial depicts the chained swan of Buckingham.

The Old Latin School on Market Hill was originally a 12th century chapel. In 1552 it was endowed as the Royal Latin School by King Edward VI.

The Manor House was built as a prebendal house of Lincoln Cathedral and is a picturesque blend of stone, timber-framing and brick infilling. The stone stack has a twisted brick chimney shaft.

Castle House is by far the most important house in the town. It has a Queen Anne facade of 1708. The original house, of which only two wings survive, was a pre-Reformation courtyard house dating from about 1500. The former Great Chamber on the first floor has a ceiling, dated 1620, with the original arch-braced collar and queenpost roof above this.

THE MARKET PLACE AND GAOL, BUCKINGHAM

THE MANOR HOUSE, BUCKINGHAM

BEAUCHAMPTON;
WHADDON; THORNTON;
THORNBOROUGH

Hall Farm, *Beauchampton*, has some good 17th century stone farm buildings with barn and stables.

Grange Farmhouse (1629) stands in Watery Lane and is a timber-framed structure on a stone base with picturesque gables and a pedimented oriel window in the jettied two-storey porch. The Old Latin School of 1668 is a two storey building of five bays with a two-storeyed gabled porch and lantern of about 1800.

Almost absorbed into the new city of Milton Keynes, the village of *Whaddon* perches on a low hill overlooking the Chase which, in the Middle Ages, was a famous deer-hunting forest. Whaddon Chase was granted by the Crown in 1242 to John FitzGeoffrey and later owned by the Giffard family and was largely cleared during the 17th century. St Mary's Church has a massively buttressed tower, 12th century arcades and a mainly 14th century exterior.

St Michael's Church, *Thornton*, is mainly 14th century.

St Mary's Church, *Thornborough*, is Early Norman, with a 13th century arcade and a late 13th century chancel.

The Old Manor House has a 14th to 15th century hall with a 16th century cross-wing, a two-storey porch and 16th century chimneystacks.

The Manor House (17th century) on The Green is of stone with a brick eaves cornice, an 18th century Doric doorcase on the east front and an early 18th century staircase and panelling. The 18th century stone watermill on the Ouse still has much of its machinery intact.

Isolated from the village over Claydon Brook is one of Buckinghamshire's treasures. The 14th century stone bridge has six arches, three cut-waters, parapets and central arches ribbed with hoodmoulds on both sides. It was by-passed in 1974 by a new road bridge.

Nearby are two Roman burial mounds from which bronze jugs, a bronze lamp, amphorae and Samian ware (2nd century AD) were excavated in 1839.

THORNBOROUGH BRIDGE

TUDOR COTTAGE, GREAT HORWOOD

THE BRICKHILLS;
NEWTON LONGVILLE;
THE HORWOODS

Bow Brickhill Church stands high on the escarpment against a backdrop of forest trees and commands panoramic views to the north-west across Milton Keynes. Remains of the Iron Age settlement of Danesborough lie in the forest to the north east of the village.

Little Brickhill was an important stop on Watling Street until the railway superseded it and its main street is lined with 18th century houses.

The tower and the chancel of St Mary's Church, *Great Brickhill*, are of the 13th century and the aisles and arcades are Perpendicular.

The Manor House in Church Lane was designed by Decimus Burton, architect of the Palm House at Kew and built in 1835.

Other noteworthy buildings include the Old Rectory (18th century), Broomhill House (1912-14), Green Farmhouse (16th century) and Cromwell Cottages.

St Faith's Church, *Newton Longville*, has a Perpendicular exterior, but the interior is largely of the 12th century with two-bay arcades of circular piers with square abaci and pointed arches.

The Manor House is early 16th century in brick with stone dressings and the Arms of New College, Oxford over the door.

The church of St James, *Great Horwood*, is remarkable for its beautiful windows with flowing tracery.

The village has several attractive Georgian houses around The Green.

Little Horwood church has some fine 13th and 14th century wall-paintings, uncovered in 1889 and depicting St Nicholas with boys pickled in a tub, the Martyrdom of Becket, part of an armoured figure and a large naked figure of Pride connected to the other Deadly Sins.

The Old Farmhouse in Church Street, one of the finest unspoilt late 16th to early 17th century timber-framed cottages in the county, has curved braces, brick infilling and a rubble-stone plinth. The roof has a gorgeous overhanging thatch and the building steps delightfully down the slope towards the road.

THE OLD FARMHOUSE, LITTLE HORWOOD

SALDEN HOUSE, MURSLEY

ADSTOCK; ADDINGTON; SWANBOURNE; PADBURY; MURSLEY

Adstock's 12th century church of St Cecilia was remodelled in the 15th century and restored in 1855.

St Mary's Church lies within the park of *Addington* Manor (1928-9) and has unusual 14th century arcades, where the piers continue into the arches without capitals. There are over sixty Netherlandish stained glass panels of the 16th and 17th centuries collected by the 1st Lord Addington in the late 19th century.

St Swithin's Church, *Swanbourne*, has a fine 13th century chancel and many Perpendicular features. A wall-painting of 1500 has Latin inscriptions and two tiers of pictures.

The Manor House in Winslow Road is Elizabethan or Jacobean. It has a doorway dated 1627 and is built of stone with gable ends, gabled dormers, mullioned and transomed windows and a three-storey porch on the east front.

Deverell's Farmhouse (1632) is also of stone and has a gabled porch projection and mullioned windows.

Padbury Main Street is lined with a fascinating collection of picturesque cottages and farmhouses, foremost among which are Glade Farmhouse (1743), College Farm, Ivy Farmhouse, Sunny Hill Farmhouse in Old End and Tithebarn, a 17th century timber-framed building on a stone base.

The church dates from the 13th century and has an extensive collection of 14th century wall-paintings.

The church of St Mary, *Mursley*, has a Jacobean pulpit and monuments to the Fortesque family of Salden, which lies about a mile to the north east. All that remains of the original mansion is the east wing, now used as a private house. It is of red brick with blue diapering over three bays and two storeys and has some stone mullioned and transomed windows on the first floor.

SWANBOURNE MANOR HOUSE

COLLEGE FARM, PADBURY

31

WINSLOW

Of Saxon origin, *Winslow* was granted by King Offa to St Albans Abbey in 795. The Abbot of St Albans laid out a new town here in the 13th century grafting it onto the existing village and a market square was established in 1235 to the south of the church of St Laurence. The church is set back from the High Street and is mostly Decorated or late 13th century.

Keach's Meeting House in Bell Walk was built in 1695 and is a simple brick building of cottage form entered from a graveyard with a high enclosing wall. The principal house in the town is Winslow Hall in Sheep Street, built in 1700-1704 for William Lowndes, Secretary to the Treasury. Probably designed by Sir Christopher Wren, the house is a stately structure on the edge of town and overlooks an open tract of countryside. Built of vitreous red brick with stone dressings, it is of superb architectural quality and has seven bays, two main floors and a half storey, a hipped roof with four large panelled chimneyshafts and moulded stone cornices. The projecting centre bay carries a pediment with a round window and the doorway has a segmental pediment.

The town focuses on the market square which has the 17th century Bell Hotel on its south side and the George Hotel on the island at the centre, with its ornate 18th century wrought-iron balcony.

Many of the surrounding buildings are timber-framed with bow windows and good shopfronts. Horn Street is worth exploration as it has several very attractive houses. Barn Studio was rebuilt by William Lowndes in 1700 and was a former tithe barn.

HORN STREET, WINSLOW

THE GEORGE HOTEL, WINSLOW

GAWCOTT; CHETWODE; HILLESDEN

Holy Trinity Church (1827), *Gawcott*, was designed by the Reverend Thomas Scott, father of Sir George Gilbert Scott, who was born here in 1811.

Westcot House in the main street was built in 1720.

The isolated and charming hamlet of *Chetwode* has a small church, which is the only surviving part of an Augustinian Priory founded in 1245.

The priory church chancel, now St Mary and St Nicholas, had a tower added and the old west wall to the demolished nave re-erected across the west end of the chancel.

Priory House lies on the site of the cloister and incorporates some of the masonry from the former priory.

The church has 13th century wall-paintings, including a tryptych with verses from the Bible and some beautiful stained glass from the same period.

Only the 18th century gateposts remain of *Hillesden's* Denton Manor, the original of which was destroyed in 1643.

All Saints Church is called 'The Cathedral in the Fields' and is an impressive building. Almost entirely Perpendicular, it has an embattled north aisle and north porch. The clerestory is a continuous band of lights. The transept and north chapel are also embattled and the two-storeyed north vestry has a stair turret with an ogee-shaped crown of openwork flying buttresses. The church was restored in 1873-75 by Sir George Gilbert Scott who was influenced, as a young local boy, by the splendour of its Gothic architecture.

HILLESDEN CHURCH IN THE FIELDS

◁ *WINSLOW HALL*

CHETWODE PRIORY CHURCH

36

THREE LOCKS, SOULBURY

STEWKLEY;
STOKE HAMMOND;
SOULBURY

The church of St Michael, *Stewkley*, is a magnificent Norman building and one of the finest examples in England of parochial architecture of the period. It is complete and was probably built between 1150 and 1180. Both interior and exterior are sumptuously decorated using typical Norman motifs. The church has a nave, a central space under the tower and a straight chancel. The west front is spectacular with a central doorway flanked by lower blank arches and an unusual tympanum, decorated with dragons with twisted tails and foliage trails. The arches have double-chevron ornament and, in the gable, there is a circular window with chevron.

The interior has a double frieze of chevron which surrounds all the windows and the two main arches to the central space have chevron and beakhead orders. The chancel has quadripartite vaulting with broad ribs banded with chevrons enclosing lozenges.

A long main street has several timber-framed and thatched houses dating from the 15th to the 17th century. Standing out amongst these are Sycamore Farmhouse (1600), numbers 78, 22 and 28 High Street, The Manor House (16th century), Dovecote Farmhouse (late 16th century), Orchard Farmhouse (16th century) and Orchard Cottage.

St Luke's, *Stoke Hammond*, is a late medieval cruciform church, built of ironstone, with fine Decorated work in the chancel windows. The font is of the 14th century on four shafts with moulded capitals.

Soulbury church was restored by Street in 1862-3 and has many monuments to the Lovetts of Liscombe Park.

Liscombe Park itself was built between 1760 and 1770 and is a two-storey brick mansion in a medieval castellated style with turrets and stepped gables.

Lovett's School on Chapel Hill was built in 1724 as a nine-bay two-storeyed building in red and vitreous brick.

Three Locks on the Grand Union canal were completed in 1812 to drop north-bound boats 20 feet.

ST. MICHAEL'S CHURCH, STEWKLEY

The Vale of Aylesbury is a broad flat plain crossing the whole county, bubbling up into low hillocks to the west, from Waddesdon to Brill, rising very gently to the north onto undulating ridges at Quainton and Whitchurch and halting abruptly against the steep, north-facing slopes of the Chilterns to the south. It follows the River Thame into Oxfordshire and fades eastwards into Bedfordshire. The Vale is best appreciated from a string of vantage points along the edge of the Chilterns, in particular from Ivinghoe Beacon, Aston Hill, Cymbeline's Castle at Ellesborough, Whiteleaf Cross and The Cop at Bledlow.

Aylesbury sits at the heart of the Vale, an isolated urban concentration which leaves surrounding villages, for the most part, unaffected and still rural in character. As the administrative centre of Buckinghamshire, the county town has greatly expanded in recent years, whilst maintaining its medieval core around the market place and church.

Amongst the villages to the north of the town, The Claydons. Whitchurch, Oving and Quainton are the most picturesque. There are important houses at Mentmore and Ascott and a remarkable Saxon church at Wing.

To the west lies Waddesdon, a striking French-style chateau crowning a prominent wooded hill. Long Crendon, Haddenham and Brill, which lie further west still, are some of the most beautiful villages in the county. Pre-eminent major houses in this region include Nether Winchendon House, Wotton House, Hartwell House, Tythrop House and the nostalgic gatehouse at Boarstall.

FROM BRILL TO WADDESDON

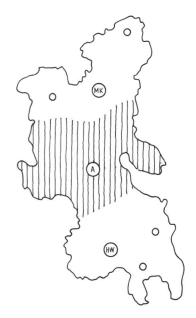

Sited on the plain in the lea of Whiteleaf Hill, Princes and Monks Risborough both have compact groups of historic buildings close to their churches but otherwise consist of rather undistinguished suburban housing. Wendover, on the other hand, has retained many of its historic buildings. These towns guard strategic gaps in the hills through which main road and railway routes pass and, in former times, were important settlements established on the Icknield Way.

A chain of bare chalk hills, including lvinghoe Beacon, dominates the landscape in an area divided from the main body of the county by a finger of Hertfordshire. In this pocket the Grand Union Canal continues to thread its way through the county.

PARSONS FEE, AYLESBURY

NORMAN DOORWAY, TWYFORD

TWYFORD; THE CLAYDONS

The Church of the Assumption, *Twyford*, has a fine Norman south doorway with zigzag and beakhead motifs in the arch. The chancel arch is also Norman. The nave roof is Perpendicular with tie-beams on arch braces, kingposts and diagonal struts. 15th century benches have poppyheads. A late 13th century monument of a cross-legged knight in Purbeck Marble lies in the south aisle.

There are many picturesque timber-framed thatched cottages in *Steeple Claydon* including Willow Vale Farmhouse (15th to 16th century) and Rhenold's Close, with 15th century cruck trusses.

Claydon House was built at *Middle Claydon* between 1750 and 1780 for the second Earl Verney, encasing a late 16th century mansion in the process and employing master carver and cabinet-maker, Luke Lightfoot, to carry out the design.

The main ground floor rooms are Palladian in character comprising The North Hall, the Pink Parlour, the Saloon and the Library and on the first floor, reached by the sumptuous staircase, are the Great Red Room, the Garland chamber, the Gothic Room and the Chinese Room. The stables date from 1754 and are set against the house.

All Saints Church stands on a small hump just south of the house and has an aisleless nave of the late 13th century and many Perpendicular additions. There are monuments to the Giffard and Verney family members.

East Claydon has several beautiful timber-framed and thatched cottages from the 16th and 17th centuries, including Jasmine cottage with its gable jettied to the street with curved braces. Almost a continuation of East Claydon to the north, *Botolph Claydon* also has some very attractive late medieval timber-framed cottages in Orchard Way, with cruck trusses. Botolph House was used as a dower house by the Verneys of Claydon and is a mid-18th century Palladian building.

COTTAGES AT BOTOLPH CLAYDON

CLAYDON HOUSE ▷

JASMINE COTTAGE, EAST CLAYDON

44

MARSH GIBBON;
GRENDON UNDERWOOD

Marsh Gibbon is a very attractive stone-built village with a fine gabled Manor House with a 16th century hall, a two-storeyed porch, timber-framed gables jettied over the bay window and porch, and wooden mullioned windows.

Cromwell House is early 17th century and unspoilt.

The Old Red Lion of 1684 is built in stone with gables and has a deep coved eaves cornice on brackets.

Swan Farmhouse (1720) is a three-bay stone house.

13th century St Mary's Church has late perpendicular windows, one in the south transept with five lights and panel tracery.

Grendon Underwood stretches for over a mile from the church of St Leonard. a fine 13th century building with several exceptional marble monuments dating from the mid-18th century.

Shakespeare Farmhouse was once an inn and is reputed to have hosted William Shakespeare for a night. It is of the late 16th century with a tall cross-wing, diagonally-braced timber-framing with brick infilling and a lower hall range. The brick chimneystack has fireplaces with three-centred arches. A painted wall panel is probably early 17th century. Other noteworthy buildings include Crucks Cottage (17th century), Minstrels Cottage (late medieval) and the Old Rectory of 1762.

THE MANOR HOUSE, MARSH GIBBON

SHAKESPEARE HOUSE, GRENDON UNDERWOOD

46

NORTH MARSTON; OVING; QUAINTON

The church of St Mary, *North Marston*, housed the shrine to John Schorne, rector from 1290 to 1314, until it was removed to Windsor by jealous Canons in 1478. He was reputed to have imprisoned the devil in a boot and the shrine and holy well attracted many pilgrims whose contributions helped to pay for the completion of St George's Chapel. The Perpendicular clerestory of large lantern-like windows is a particularly attractive feature of the church.

St John's Manor has a 16th century close-studded front wing with curved braces and brick and lath and plaster infill. The 14th century rear wing has a cruck truss.

Oving House was built in the early 17th century and remodelled in 1743.

The main street of this picturesque little village runs between Oving House and the church of All Saints, and is lined by 17th and 18th century cottages and grassy verges. The timber-framed and brick infilled Black Boy Inn terminates the vista at the north end.

Quainton stands on a prominent hill looking south towards Waddesdon, with cottages and farms grouped around a large green.

Towering over the green is the windmill of 1830, now restored and equipped with sails.

The church of St Mary and Holy Cross stands at the eastern extremity of the village and has several fine monuments to the Dormer family.

Adjacent to the churchyard entrance are the Winwood Almshouses which date from 1687. Opposite the almshouses stands Brudenell House with its 18th century facade screening 16th century ranges.

Other houses of note along Church Street include Banner Farmhouse (17th century), numbers 24 to 26 (dated 1722) and number 2 (early 16th century).

The village cross is 15th century and behind it stands Cross Farmhouse of 1723 in chequered brick with the Dormer Arms in a stone cartouche.

NORTH MARSTON CHURCH

THE WINWOOD ALMSHOUSES, QUAINTON

WHITCHURCH; CUBLINGTON

The earthworks of Bolbec Castle (1147), *Whitchurch*, lie in the village just west of Market Hill.

St John the Evangelist Church has a fine, intact, 13th century chancel and 14th century arcades.

The tower was built within the west end of the nave, cutting into the arcades.

The village has many attractive houses worth close examination. In High Street, Priory Hotel is a 15th century timber-framed house with brick infilling on a stone base. The upper floor is oversailing and the chimneys are on the diagonal.

Old House in Church Headland Lane has a 15th century core and was remodelled both in the 17th and 20th centuries. The north front is of stone with an oversailing upper storey of timber-framing.

Other noteworthy houses include Kempson House (late 17th century) and numbers 28 and 58 High Street. 16th century number 49 has a jettied upper storey.

At *Cublington*, the motte of a Norman Castle lies a quarter of a mile to the west of St Nicholas Church, which replaced an earlier church sited close to the castle and the vanished village.

Neale's Farm is of 1600 with timber-framing and brick infill. The early 17th century staircase has turned balusters.

OLD HOUSE, WHITCHURCH

ASCOTT; WING; MENTMORE; WINGRAVE

Located just to the east of Wing, the origin[al] *Ascott* House, which has disappeared entirel[y] was the home of the Dormers. The house w[as] ransacked during the Civil War and became [a] ruin. The present house started out as a mode[st] timber-framed house, dated 1606, and wa[s] bought by Baron Mayer de Rothschild in 187[3]. The subsequently enlarged house retained the ol[d] part at the centre and the black and whit[e] appearance dates from the late 1930s.

The church of All Saints, *Wing*, is one of th[e] most important Anglo-Saxon monuments i[n] England. It has a polygonal apse, a crypt an[d] aisles and is a pre-Conquest structure. The nave[,] north aisle and first phase of the crypt ar[e] probably of the early 9th century. The apse i[s] articulated externally by tall pilaster-strips at the angles of the seven sides and these carry thin arches like blind arcading. The pilaster strip[s] continue upwards and carry triangular heads similar to details at Earls Barton in Northamptonshire. All this Anglo-Saxon work is of the 10th century. In the nave, three bays of the arcades are also Anglo-Saxon. The roof is a 15th century tie-beam structure incorporating saints and kings and, on the wall-plate below the kingposts, are angels with outstretched wings. The Dormer monuments include a fine Renaissance example to Sir Robert who died in 1552.

Mentmore House was designed by Sir Joseph Paxton and built between 1850 and 1855 for Baron Mayer Amschel de Rothschild. The Roseberys owned the house from 1878 but in 1977 the fine family collections were auctioned off.

The stone house stands prominently on a hill overlooking undulating countryside to the west. Influenced by Wollaton in Nottinghamshire, it has similar square angle towers.

The central hall has a glass roof built on Paxton's ridge and furrow principle.

Wingrave's Church Farmhouse is dated 1793 and 1828, but the outer cloak of brick conceals a late 15th or early 16th century house with three cruck trusses. It also has a chimneystack dated 1600 and a stone fireplace of 1619.

ASCOTT HOUSE

The chancel of St Peter and St Paul Church dates entirely from about 1190 and has blank wall arcading on north and south sides. The nave arcades were built in the 14th century.

Other buildings to note in the village include Windmill House (18th century). Mount Tabor House (1870s), Floyd's Farmhouse in Mill Lane (17th century timber-framing) and Dene Leys in Nup End Lane (late 16th century).

MENTMORE HOUSE

51

CHURCH OF ALL SAINTS, WING

SLAPTON;
EDLESBOROUGH;
CHEDDINGTON

Slapton church has a Perpendicular exterior masking a 14th century nave and chancel. The Carpenter's Arms is of the 17th century in timber-framing and thatch.

One mile to the south at Horton is a rectangular moat around Horton Hall, once the manor house with a chapel.

The large embattled church of St Mary, *Edlesborough*, dominates the flat landscape to the west as it stands on a prominent and isolated hill. It is now redundant but boasts fine 13th century arcades, a tower of the same period with a stair turret and twinned bell-openings. The Perpendicular pulpit has a rare four-tier canopy.

Church Farm has a 180 foot long 15th to 16th century Tithebarn in timber-framing and brick infilling, which has now been converted to offices.

A nearby Dovecote (mid-18th century) is square with four gables and 350 nesting boxes.

There are several interesting old houses overlooking The Green at *Cheddington*, including The Chase (1500).

In the High Street The Old Reading Room and The Swan pub are of the 17th century. Norman fragments of the church of St Giles can be seen in the porch, nave and vestry.

EDLESBOROUGH CHURCH

DAGNALL; IVINGHOE; PITSTONE; MARSWORTH

One of the most important International Modern houses in the country sits high up on the escarpment above *Dagnall*. Hillfield, by Berthold Lubetkin, was built between 1933 and 1936 for himself, and was designed for open-air living. The single-storey house is constructed of in situ concrete, has long continuously glazed walls and sits comfortably on its site almost entirely screened by stands of beech trees, which continue over the hill behind to the edge of Whipsnade Zoo. The house has recently been renovated and painted starkly white.

St Mary's Church, *Ivinghoe*, is a large, embattled 13th century cruciform building, whose tower was added in the early 14th century. Amongst its monuments is a rare stone effigy of a priest, under a recess in the chancel, dating from about 1300.

The King's Head is a 16th century timber-framed structure behind a brick frontage. Other noteworthy buildings include the Old Vicarage (I8th century), the Old Brewery House (I800),the Town Hall (late I6th century with Victorian modifications), Pendyce House,with its hall of 1300 and Ford End Farm Watermill (1798), which is now a museum and has a weatherboarded upper floor and complete machinery.

The hillfort on lvinghoe Beacon is thought to date from the 9th century BC.

The church of St Mary at *Pitstone* stands alone at Church End but was once at the centre of the vanished village. It dates from 1230, when the chancel was built, was rebuilt during the 15th century and restored in 1892-3. A wall-painting of 1733 fills the upper wall of the nave east wall. Pitstone Green Windmill lies between Pitstone and Ivinghoe and is a restored post-mill dating from 1627. It has a circular brick base, a weatherboarded chamber above, four sails and 19th century machinery.

Marsworth has a good canalscape with locks and bridges of about I800, a lock-keeper's cottage and a pumping station.

PITSTONE MILL

54

THE KINGS HEAD, IVINGHOE

HULCOTT; BIERTON; DRAYTON BEAUCHAMP; BUCKLAND

Hulcott has an attractive tree-fringed green around which a number of Rothschild estate cottages cluster, built in the 1860s by Devey. He also altered the 17th century Manor House which retains its original staircase with contemporary wall paintings on its upper walls. All Saints Church dates from the 13th century and has a 16th century timber support within the nave, for the bellcote and shingled spire.

St James Church, Bierton, is almost entirely 14th century and has some fragments of contemporary wall paintings in the south aisle. A mile to the south the hamlet of Broughton has Old Manor Farmhouse, a 17th century timber-framed house incorporating a 15th century hall house and outlines of a double moat nearby suggest the site of the manor.

The embattled outline of St Mary's Church, *Drayton Beauchamp*, greets the visitor approaching along a field footpath. The church is isolated from the village and stands close to a closed-off and dry section of the Wendover arm of the Grand Union Canal. All windows are Perpendicular, and there is a fine pair of brasses to two knights, William and Thomas Cheyne, who died in 1375 and 1368 respectively.

Moat Farm (16th century), *Buckland*, is timber-framed but has now been stuccoed. The barn has four cruck trusses. The Canal Bridge at Buckland Wharf (1811-13) has a round brick arch and outswept parapet. All Saints Church has a late 11th century north arcade and a 14th century doorway but was heavily restored during Victorian times.

ST MARY'S CHURCH, DRAYTON BEAUCHAMP

AYLESBURY

There was settlement at *Aylesbury* during the Iron Age and a small Roman community may have fronted Akeman Street. The town grew by the 10th century to include a mint, a market and a Royal Manor.

From 1218 onwards the assizes were frequently held here instead of at Buckingham.

The town is still compact and based upon its medieval street plan, although the centre has shifted from Kingsbury to the Market Square. During the 16th and 17th centuries, prosperity derived from the fertile Vale of Aylesbury but in the 18th century, lace-making became the most important industry and, during this period, many of the timber-framed houses were refronted in brick.

In the latter half of the 19th century other industries moved into the town and by the l930s light engineering became predominant. The coming of the railways to Aylesbury in the late 1800s caused rapid growth and, by the 1960s, the population was over 40,000. St Mary's Church is a large cruciform building of the 13th and 14th centuries which was heavily restored during the Victorian period by Sir George Gilbert Scott. It stands in a leafy churchyard at the head of Church Street and has a rather cavernous interior. County Hall was built on the Market Square from 1722 until 1740 and is Palladian in form. Of seven bays and two storeys in red brick, with the middle three bays carrying a pediment crowned by three stone vases. the building encloses the south side of the Market Square. St Mary's Square is surrounded by 15th century facades fronting older buildings. Opening off Parson's Fee is the arched 18th century gateway to the Prebendal House, which was built for William Mead, a London merchant, altered in the 1750s by politician John Wilkes and again in 1825 by Thomas Tindall.

Church Street has some of the town's finest houses. Hickman's Almshouses were established in 1695 and rebuilt in 1871. The former Grammar School is now the County Museum and was built in 1720. Ceely House has a fine 18th century facade in red brick concealing a 15th century timber-framed building, erected as the Brotherhood House of the Fraternity of the Virgin Mary. The interior has the original roof structure and one room has an important scheme of painted decoration on the plaster.

The 17th century Chantry has a stuccoed front dated 1830-40, with bargeboarded gables and ogee-headed, octagon-paned windows, some with portrait heads as keystones. Castle Street is lined with neat 18th century fronted houses, those on one side standing above the road which was lowered during the 19th century.

A fine 18th century wrought-iron sign across a narrow passage on the north side marks the presence of the King's Head Hotel, built in the 15th century and extended in the 16th and 17th centuries. It has three gabled bays, the left-hand one of which belongs to the 15th century hall range. with a large window of twenty lights. The upper lights have four-centred arched heads and stained glass with angels bearing the arms of Henry VI and Margaret of Anjou. The whole building is a delight, with timber beams, a moulded timber gate arch to the yard and a late 17th century staircase open to the gate-passage. The building is timber-framed around two sides of the courtyard and, in the room over the gate, is an open timber queenpost roof of the 16th century with windbraces. Kingsbury, the original town market square. has some interesting old buildings, including the 16th century Lobster Pot with its jettied upper floor to Pebble Lane and its rare hammerbeam roof, and the Red Lion of about 1600.

THE KING'S HEAD, AYLESBURY

CASTLE STREET, AYLESBURY

KINGSBURY, AYLESBURY

59

WADDESDON

Waddesdon Manor is an elaborate and flamboyant French-style chateau which dominates the surrounding gentle landscape from its prominent hilltop site. Built for Baron Ferdinand de Rothschild between 1877 and 1883 to the design of Destailleur, it borrows freely from the chateaux of Blois and Chambord on the Loire. Of Bath stone, it is two storeys high with dormers reminiscent of Azay-le-Rideau and Chenonceau. The entrance porch incorporates a porte-cochere and the house bristles with tall chimneys, domed towers and steep roofs. The Garden Front has eleven bays. Close to the house, the gardens are formal, but fall enticingly away through sweeping vales and stands of fine trees. On the approach side is a wide avenue lined by formally planted trees and introduced by a fountain with 18th century figures of a triton, nereids and sea-monsters. The house is now owned and run by the National Trust.

WADDESDON MANOR

60

FOUNTAIN AT WADDESDON MANOR

61

LUDGERSHALL; WOTTON UNDERWOOD

St Mary's Church, *Ludgershall*, has a 14th century chancel and arcades built soon afterwards. The two-storey porch and west tower are Perpendicular. The chancel has a hammer-beam roof with pendants dated about 1500.

Wotton Underwood church stands about 300 meters away from Wotton House, for whose owners it became a mortuary chapel after 1710. There is a fine black marble slab with a brass to Edward Greneveile (died 1585) and his wife. There is a range of luminous stained glass coats of arms in the family chapel, of about 1800, made by Francis Eginton.

Wotton House was built for Richard Grenville between 1704 and 1714. The Grenvilles later became the Dukes of Buckingham. The house takes the form of a central block with two independent pavilions linked to the house by quadrant walls. After a fire, Soane reconstructed the house in 1821-22 for the 2nd Marquess and much of his work has, in recent years, been painstakingly restored by the owner, the late Mrs Brunner. Of brick with stone dressings, the house has eleven bays and two storeys It has giant Corinthian pilasters at the angles and at the angles of the three-bay centre. On the parapet there are fine 18th century stone urns and figures. The west front is the same but of nine bays with the centre faced in rusticated stone. The building is crowned by a row of bold rectangular chimneystacks. The entrance front has a forecourt with low walls which lead to the two flanking pavilions, the Clock Pavilion containing the kitchen and the South Pavilion, which contained the coach house. The forecourt is closed by a magnificent wrought-iron screen, gates and overthrow, attributed to Thomas Robinson. The Saloon, Dining Room and Drawing Room have retained their 18th century character.

WOTTON HOUSE

ASHENDON;
CHEARSLEY;
CUDDINGTON;
LOWER WINCHENDON;
UPPER WINCHENDON;

St Mary's Church, *Ashendon*, has Norman remnants and a fine 13th century nave arch and Perpendicular clerestory windows. A defaced late 13th century effigy of a cross-legged knight lies under a 15th century ogee arch.

South-east of the *Chearsley* church is the rectangular moat of a medieval manor house with fishponds nearby. St Nicholas has elements of 13th, 14th and 15th century building and a west gallery, dated 1761, with timber-framed windows.

Cuddington clusters around a small green on the Chearsley to Dinton road and is surrounded by small witchert cottages. Upper Church street is also lined with cottages and has Bernard Hall (1933-34), a strange but picturesque timber-framed building. with brick infill and a stone base.

St Nicholas Church has a Norman nave arcade with fine capitals of trumpet scalloping and a chancel arch with roll mouldings.

The church of *Lower Winchendon* has a 15th century tower with a higher stair turret and a 13th century chancel. The box-pews (19th century) and the pulpit (1613) are attractive features.

The somewhat bizarre and intriguing exterior of Nether Winchendon House reflects a long history going back to 1162, when the property was granted by the Earl of Buckingham to the newly founded monastery of Notley, situated only three miles away. It is a striking composition of brickwork with stone dressings, battlements, tall twisted chimney stacks and stone towers and stands in an idyllic situation on the banks of the River Thame. Parts of the original house are incorporated into the present building. which was first remodelled after 1527 by Sir John Daunce, a Privy Councillor to King Henry VIII. He added the east wing and the beautiful Drawing Room with its superb linenfold wall panelling and fretted oak frieze. It was substantially altered by Sir Scrope Bernard

CUDDINGTON COTTAGE

between 1793 and 1803 in the Gothick style, when he added the Entrance Hall, Morning Room, stone corner towers to the east range and the stone screen to the entrance forecourt. He also renewed the cupola over the south range, adding an ogee cap, created the Justice Room and remodelled the Great Hall, where he designed the plaster vaulted ceiling.

The house is still owned and occupied by descendants of Sir Francis Bernard who inherited in 1771.

Upper Winchendon church and Manor house overlook the vale northwards towards Waddesdon, and the village is strung out along the relatively high ridge with plunging slopes to either side and ravishing views of the Chilterns to the south-east. St Mary Magdalene has a Norman nave and north aisle and the wooden pulpit dates from the 14th century.

NETHER WINCHENDON HOUSE

THE BELL, CHEARSLEY

BOARSTALL; BRILL; DORTON; CHILTON

Boarstall Tower is all that survives of a large 13th to 14th century moated house, which was demolished in the late 18th century. It has canted bay windows on the sides and a late 16th century fireplace in the room over the gate arch. The two-arched brick moat bridge dates from 1736. The gatehouse is now a private house, and the central passage has been made into a room.

Tower Farmhouse is early 17th century, of brick in two storeys with mullioned windows. The village of *Brill* crowns a very distinctive hill, commanding views over the Vale of Aylesbury to the east and towards Oxford in the west.

The Green and The Square dictate the layout of the village. Edward the Confessor had a house here, which he no doubt used when hunting in Bernwood Forest. The church may have been the royal chapel.

Brill was a centre of clay-based industries, including pottery, tile and brick manufacture, lasting well into the 20th century and reflected in the pitted landscape of the common. Many pottery kilns dating from the 14th century onwards have been excavated in the village. All Saints was originally an aisleless Norman church and has a 12th century east window of four lights. The tower was added in the 15th century.

Noteworthy buildings in the village include Brill House (18th century) on The Green, The Manor House (17th century) in The Square and the Old Vicarage (1773). The Windmill is the last survivor of six which originally existed in Brill. Built in the 1680s, it has a low brick roundhouse, with a weatherboarded post mill complete with sails.

Dorton House is a large 17th century mansion of red brick with stone dressings built for Sir John Dormer. The Hall has original panelling and the staircase has a date of 1626 in the stucco work. The Great Chamber has a coved ceiling with sinuous straps and the Dormer emblem. A barrel-vaulted Long Gallery runs the length of the first floor of the north wing.

BRILL MILL

The church of St Mary, *Chilton*, has a 13th century chancel with single lancets and three stepped lancets at the east end. The two-storey porch has a tunnel vault. A large alabaster monument to Sir John Croke (died 1608) has two recumbent figures and detached kneeling figures against the front of the tomb chest.

Chilton House (1740) is a remodelling of an earlier Croke house, incorporating some 16th century remnants, including the Long Gallery with its barrel-vaulted ceiling and linenfold panelling.

Townhill Farm is 17th century and other fine buildings include Wheelwrights in Church Road, with its medieval hall truss in the gable and jettied cross-wing, The Gatehouse (1683), and Chilton Park Farmhouse (1609).

BOARSTALL TOWER

CHILTON COTTAGES

WORMINGHALL; ICKFORD; SHABBINGTON

Worminghall church has a Norman south doorway, a 12th century chancel arch, a 14th century chancel and a 15th century tower.

The Almshouses in The Avenue were founded in 1675. Clifden Arms has two cruck trusses in a medieval wing. The Homesteads (16th century) is a typical thatched, timber-framed cottage.

St Nicholas Church. *Ickford*, is a beautiful 12th to 13th century building with a saddleback tower roof standing in a secluded and wooded churchyard. The monument to Thomas Tipping (died 1595) has nine children kneeling against the big tomb-chest. The inscription plate has a strapwork surround with figures in North American Indian head-dresses.

The 16th century Old Rectory is timber-framed. although remodelled in brick and stone. Church Farmhouse is 17th century with one medieval cruck truss, and there are further crucks in College Cottage in Worminghall Road.

Ickford Bridge, over the River Thame, is medieval with alterations dated 1685, and has three stone arches.

There is some early Norman work in *Shabbington* church and a low Perpendicular tower with battlements. The nave roof has unusual rough tie-beams and queenposts.

THE HOMESTEADS, WORMINGHALL

LONG CRENDON;
NOTLEY ABBEY

Situated just two miles north of Thame in Oxfordshire, *Long Crendon* is a large and once prosperous village. During the medieval period, it had a successful wool trade and was known in later centuries for needle-making and lace-making.

There are many medieval houses of cruck construction and later houses of witchert, stone and brick. The long High Street has a series of ends leading off it but much of the newer village is strung out along the main through road.

St Mary's Early English style church has a tall Perpendicular crossing tower and 15th century chancel roof.

Close to the church stands the Court House (15th century), which hosted the annual manor court in the first floor room which extended the length of the building. It has an open queenpost roof with three trusses. The building has a stone base and an oversailing timber-framed upper floor with brick infilling. The east end is recessed but the roof continues over, supported on arch braces in the Wealden style.

In the High Street there are many fine picturesque thatched cottages and two larger houses of particular note. Madges has an 18th century chequered brick front and an adjoining 16th century timber-framed structure, whose thatched roof spans a carriageway and the barn beyond. Thompson's Farm (15th to 16th century) is partly timber-framed with brick and stone elements and has a large stack with diagonally set chimneys.

Along Bicester Road, Sycamore Farm has a 13th century aisled hall with a cruck truss and there are several other late medieval houses scattered nearby.

At Lower End, both The Old Crown (late 16th century) and Dragon Farm House (mid-16th century) are former inns.

Long Crendon Manor, in Frogmore Lane, is a magnificent 14th to 16th century house, with a 15th century stone gatehouse buttressed against the street. Built partly of stone and partly of timber-framing, it contains a hall with an arch-braced cruck truss and two wings. Extensive remodelling took place in 1918, altering its appearance enormously, but the whole building is still a stunning composition. A unique thatch-capped witchert wall connects two garden summerhouses.

Notley Abbey was dissolved under the Dissolution in 1538 and the church was destroyed. However, substantial parts of the domestic buildings remain. It was founded for Augustinian canons in 1162 as the Abbey of St Mary the Virgin and St John the Baptist, by Walter Giffard, the 2nd Earl of Buckingham. In 1730 it became a farm.

The Abbot's Lodging (15th century) is in the farmhouse and the house contains the Abbot's Hall, the Parlour and the Solar to its west. At the north-west angle is a fine stone stair turret. In the roof space are the remains of a decorative wall-painting (16th century) showing floral sprays growing out of a knot.

The church had a crossing and transept, a cloister, chapter house and refectory of which some beautiful 13th century arcading remains in the south range.

The square stone dovecote (16th to 17th century) has a hipped roof on queenpost trusses, and walls filled with nesting boxes divide the internal space into four rooms.

Notley Abbey is a magical place approached along an avenue of limes hanging low overhead and planted by the former owners and residents, Laurence Olivier (later Sir Laurence) and his second wife, Vivienne Leigh.

LONG CRENDON MANOR

LONG CRENDON COURT HOUSE

HADDENHAM; DINTON; ASTON SANDFORD; KINGSEY

Haddenham has three greens and stretches for almost a mile from south to north. The Ends are linked by two parallel streets. Townside and Churchway.

The churchyard of St Mary is lapped by the waters of the pond at Church End. Around the green are several fine houses, including Manor Farmhouse with its 15 to 16th century stone-encased timber-framed range, Church Farmhouse (15th century), a Wealden-type structure reminiscent of the Court House at Long Crendon, and Church End Cottage.

The church has 13th century tower, chancel and arcades. The font is Norman of the Aylesbury type and the benches are late medieval with poppyheads.

Other noteworthy buildings include Grenville Manor (15th century), with a stone front of 1781, Orchard Dene, a thatched 16th century hall with wall paintings, Oak Beam Cottage, a 15th century cruck-frame house and, in Townside. The Turn, by Aldington and Craig, completed in 1968 around a shared courtyard with mono-pitched, tiled roofs and white rendered walls. There are many examples of witchert walls in Townsend.

Dinton Church has an outstanding Norman doorway with spiral shafts, chevron and billet mouldings, a lintel with a dragon about to eat St Michael and a tympanum with two beasts eating fruit from a Tree of Life.

Dinton Hall (started 1500) stands next to the church and is remarkable for its forest of chimneys and gables.

The tiny church of St Michael, *Aston Sandford*, has a weatherboarded bell-tower and a stained glass seated Christ of the late 13th century in the east window.

Tythrop House, *Kingsey*, was built by the younger son of the fourth Earl of Pembroke, James Herbert. It is a 1676 remodelling of an early 17th century house, which itself has an older 16th century core. Of red brick with stone dressings, the Carolian house is of three storeys and has nine bays on the south garden front. The roof is hipped with dormers and a timber modillion cornice. The interior has several fine features including the late 17th century staircase by Edward Pierce, rich plasterwork on the ceilings by the Morris family and the Francini brothers, and particularly beautiful chimneypieces in the Drawing Room and the east and west rooms on the ground floor.

The parterre garden is enclosed by a haha, separating it from a delightful open field landscape.

HADDENHAM CHURCH AND POND

◁ *NOTLEY ABBEY*

73

CHURCH FARMHOUSE, HADDENHAM

TYTHROP HOUSE, KINGSEY

STONE; HARTWELL

The village of *Stone* straggles along the main road, but the church stands in a picturesque group of old brick and witchert houses to the south and has a 14th century tower, a 13th century chancel with lancets and transepts and a Norman south doorway, with chevron arch motifs. The cylindrical font is also Norman, with five panels decorated with heads, beasts and other symbols. The benches are medieval with poppyheads.

The Village Hall was designed in 1911 by Clough Williams-Ellis in Classical and Arts and Crafts style.

Hartwell House lies just to the east of Stone and is an early 17th century mansion built by Sir Alexander Hampden, who inherited it in 1570 and died in 1617. In 1690, Sir Thomas Lee laid out the elaborate garden for which Gibbs designed several buildings and monuments during the 1730s including the Ionic Temple, the Gothic Tower and the Obelisk. The only part of the house he managed to complete was the Great Hall. The house is of stone with two storeys and a parapet and was remodelled, in Classical style, by Henry Keene. The north front has a square central porch. Over this is a large oriel window lighting the Great Chamber. The Hall has magnificent stuccowork and a lavish chimneypiece. The Grand Staircase is Jacobean in style and the Drawing Room has a Rococo plaster ceiling. The house was extensively and successfully remodelled by Eric Throssel during the 1980s for its present function as a hotel. The church of St Mary is now just a shell and was designed by Henry Keene in 1753 in Gothic Revival style. The octagonal core is flanked by identical towers and it stands very prominently on a mound just to the north west of Hartwell House.

HARTWELL HOUSE, THE BRIDGE AND THE CHURCH

WESTON TURVILLE; WENDOVER

The old part of *Weston Turville* lies away from the Icknield Way, where the church of St Mary and the early Georgian Manor House are situated. In the Manor grounds are the remains of a substantial motte.

Wendover is situated at a strategic gap in the Chilterns on the London to Aylesbury route.

The church and manor house stand apart at the southern edge of town. The High Street falls to the east, focussed on the Clocktower building, and is lined with 18th century brick and timber-framed buildings. St Mary's Church is largely 14th century, although much restored.

The Clocktower of 1842 was built as a market hall, but in 1870 the brick tower with timber belfry and spire were added. The east side of Aylesbury Road is contained by a terrace of fine 15th century houses. The Old Corner House is a former coaching inn, The Old Cottage has its upper floor jettied out over the pavement and Old Manor Farmhouse is a late 16th century timber-framed house with hall and chamber wing. Other fine houses include The Red House, Sturrick House, Chiltern House, The Old House and The Grange. Castle House is of 1800 and has cast-iron balconies and the Rothschild monogram. Coldharbour lies in Tring road, and is a picturesque terrace of 17th century thatched and timber-framed cottages terminated at the upper end by the Packhorse pub.

In the High Street the Literary Institute of 1863 by William Wilkinson is in the High Victorian style, and the Red Lion (1669) has a fine mock-Tudor facade of 1900. Together, the Old Post Office and Bosworth House make up a fine timber-framed house of the 16th century, with its upper east end floor jettied. Remnants of 16th century wall-paintings can be seen in first floor rooms.

THE CLOCK TOWER, WENDOVER

Vine Tree Farmhouse in Back Street is early 18th century. Limetree House in Pound Street is mid-Georgian and is a very attractive three-bay house with Venetian windows.

The Old Mill House in Hale Road is an 18th century weatherboarded watermill converted in 1923 into a house.

COLDHARBOUR, WENDOVER

CHURCH HILL COTTAGES, ELLESBOROUGH

ELLESBOROUGH; GREAT KIMBLE

Ellesborough is one of the most picturesquely sited of the county's villages standing on a mound overlooking the Vale of Aylesbury to the north and in turn, overlooked from the slopes of Cymbeline's Mount, the site of a medieval motte and bailey castle.

The church of St Peter and St Paul has a tall tower with stair-turret, a 14th century south arcade and much Victorian restoration work. Church Hill Cottages nestle into the hillside below. Lady Dodd's Cottages are single storey brick almshouses on Church Hill built in 1746.

The Victorian exterior of *Great Kimble* church disguises an interior of 13th century arcades and an early 14th century chancel arch. The font is Norman and there are medieval tiles reset in the north chapel walls.

Timber-framed Old Grange stands within a moated site has a 15th century hall with elaborate central truss and a group of 18th century weatherboarded and stone barns.

Pulpit Hill is a well-preserved Iron Age hill-fort sited on the scarp above the village.

PRINCES RISBOROUGH; MONKS RISBOROUGH

Princes Risborough lies in a gap in the Chilterns and was a Royal Manor from the time of Domesday until 1628. In the early 14th century, Edward, the Black Prince, had a stud farm here and the moated site of the royal house was partly excavated in 1955.

The Manor House was built between 1630 and 1650. Of red brick and five bays wide over two storeys, it has a hipped roof and brick pilasters separating the bays.

Monks Staithe is a 15th to 16th century house with a timber-frame, brick infilling and a massive end stack. Church Street has several early buildings including one 15th century house with a long jettied front.

The Market House was rebuilt in 1824 as a cornmarket. It is square and of brick with open arches on the ground floor and a 19th century timber veranda on three sides. The pyramid roof has a bell-turret with a tented cap.

St Dunstan's Church, *Monks Risborough*, is of the 14th and 15th centuries and was restored by Street in 1863. The clerestory lights are particularly elegant.

Buildings of interest include the Old Rectory of 1670, a square stone 16th century Dovecote off Mill Lane, several picturesque timber-framed cottages in Burton Lane and The Bell House in Crowbrook Road, a timber-framed house with 16th century cross-wing, a 17th century hall range and an 18th century rear wing in brick.

THE MARKET HALL, PRINCES RISBOROUGH

The Chilterns have come to symbolise the landscape of Buckinghamshire, their steep northern face either crowned with stands of beech trees or starkly bare. The ancient Icknield Way was sited at the foot of the escarpment and there are several hillforts and round barrows strung along the ridge, notably at Ivinghoe Beacon, Whiteleaf, Ellesborough and Bledlow.

Once on the chalky high ground, one enters a maze of narrow country lanes connecting scattered hamlets, bottoms, greens and commons, made up of cottages and farmhouses. There are few complete villages up here but, in two places, the Chilterns are pierced by major valleys running in a south easterly direction, carrying main roads and railways towards the capital, and this is where we find several attractive settlements, including the Missendens and Bradenham. The nearer one gets to Chesham, Amersham and High Wycombe, the more suburban the settlements become, as fingers of new housing push up into the countryside.

Of the market towns, Old Amersham is the best preserved, its elegant main street lined with houses and inns dating from the fifteenth century onwards and punctuated by its magnificent freestanding market hall. Both Chesham and High Wycombe have succumbed to redevelopment and expansion whilst retaining only fragments of their historic centres. Beaconsfield also has an attractive old quarter based around four distinct ends, but has mushroomed into a substantial commuter town and, whilst the Chalfonts have remained small and village-like, their near neighbour, Gerrards Cross, fulfils all the Metroland criteria identified by John Betjeman.

NEAR WHITELEAF

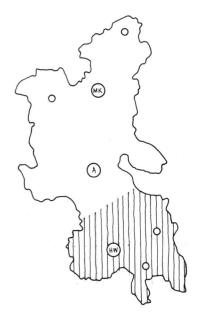

There is a pocket of glorious wooded farmland contained between the M40 and the Thames and here, the villages of Ibstone, Turville, Fingest and Hambleden remain quite unspoilt, in a landscape laced with footpaths and offering some of the best walking in the county.

The Thames is enchanting from Medmenham through Marlow to Cliveden. Inland, at Burnham Beeches, there are substantial areas of former hunting forest and, on the fringes of Slough, which is now in Berkshire, important historic locations include Stoke Poges churchyard, made eternally famous by poet Thomas Gray, and Dorney Court, one of the finest Tudor manorhouses in England.

THE THAMES AT CLIVEDEN

82

BLEDLOW; RADNAGE; STOKENCHURCH

RADNAGE CHURCH

Bledlow stands at the foot of the Chiltern scarp and its parish has a number of Iron Age and Roman sites. The Lyde is a wooded ravine landscaped in the 1980s for Lord Carrington of the Manor House, as a garden for the villagers.

Holy Trinity Church is at Church End and is a flint 13th century building, with fragments of Norman work lying in the north aisle. There are wall-paintings of the 15th century and some 14th century heraldic stained glass in a south aisle window.

The Manor House was built in 1670 and has later additions and modifications made by the Carrington family. Lyde End by Aldington and Craig (1975-77) is an attractive group of mono-pitched houses around a court. Manor Cottage and Church End Cottage are 16th and 17th century timber-framed structures. In West Lane, The Cottage is 15th century with cruck trusses.

To the south of the village lies Old Callow Down Farmhouse, a late 15th or early 16th century house with crucks.

Bledlow Cross, of unknown date, is cut in the chalk on Wain Hill.

The solid looking church of St Mary, *Radnage*, stands in this picturesque fold in the Chilterns. The tower is central and of 1200 with lancets. The tie-beam roof has traceried spandrels of the 15th century. There are wall-paintings of the 13th and 15th centuries and some interesting texts dating from the 16th to the 18th centuries.

Stokenchurch is bisected by the main Oxford to High Wycombe road and has a small church of Norman origin with a shingled bell-turret. The chancel arch is Norman, the nave dates from the early 13th century and there are two 15th century brasses to local knights.

BRADEHHAM;
LACEY GREEN;
GREAT HAMPDEN;
CHEQUERS

Bradenham church and the manor stand at the head of a generous open Green lined by largely 18th century houses set against a rising backdrop of woodland.

St Botolph's has Norman beginnings, an aisleless nave and a Perpendicular tower. The chantry chapel dates from 1542.

Bradenham Manor is an impressive late 17th century house built of red brick with a hipped roof and dormers of about 1860. The west front has eight bays over two storeys and a simple rusticated door surround. The forecourt is enclosed by a wall with gatepiers and wrought-iron gates.

North of *Lacey Green* church stands a timber-framed and weatherboarded smock mill of 1650, renovated by the Chiltern Society (1971-83) and given sails and a fantail. Above the brick base the mill is a four-storeyed, octagonal, sloping-sided shape, with the windows set like raking dormers. It has a weatherboarded curving cap and the machinery, mill stones and gear are all intact.

Great Hampden lies high in the Chilterns, which are threaded by narrow lanes and largely covered with mature forest.

Hampden House was built around a medieval core by John Hampden in the mid-18th century and is a remarkable early example of the Gothick style.

St Mary Magdalene Church, which stands at the end of a glorious avenue of limes, is of flint with a predominantly Perpendicular exterior, although there are 13th century arcades and tower arches. The benches are early Tudor with linenfold panels.

A fine former chair-bodger's cottage with an enormous overhanging thatched roof stands in a cluster of buildings opposite the village pub at the heart of the village.

Well-preserved lengths of Grim's Ditch survive about half a mile north west of Hampden House.

BRADENHAM MANOR

The flint rubble church of *Little Hampden* has a 13th century nave and wall-paintings of the same period. The 15th century two-storey north porch has a timber frame with louvred openings in its belfry.

Chequers is the country seat of British Prime Ministers and is a mid-16th century manor built by William Hawtrey. The north front is eight bays wide over two storeys, with an additional attic storey and five gables rising from a parapet. The Hawtrey Room has 16th century panelling, as does the Great Parlour.

The walled south garden has a parterre with summerhouses at the corners and the house looks out onto a stunning landscape of fields enclosed by forest-clad hills.

FORMER CHAIR-BODGER'S COTTAGE, GREAT HAMPDEN

THE MISSENDENS; HUGHENDEN

Great Missenden church is now separated from the village by the bypass road and stands on a high bank, flanked by fine beech trees. Many of its features are in the Decorated style but the tower is Perpendicular, as are the nave roof and the clerestory. The roof has arched braces resting on stone angels with tracery in the spandrels.

The village street is a densely packed collection of 16th to 17th century houses and inns, mostly with 18th to 19th century facades and the whole picture is very attractive.

Missenden Abbey stands at the south end and was founded in 1133 as an Arroasian House for Augustinian Canons.

Abbey Farmhouse was the former gatehouse to the Abbey, much altered in the 18th century. The George inn has a 15th to 16th century hall and parlour wing and a barn at the rear of the same period, with its roof bracketed out over an external stair.

The most attractive way to approach *Little Missenden* is along the narrow lane from Beamond End which finally descends to the village, sitting enticingly in the lush Misbourne valley.

St John the Baptist has a Saxon and early Norman interior with several fine wall-paintings. The roof timbers are crude but suit the rather similar interior with its unmoulded 12th century nave arches.

Adjacent to the church, the Manor House is a large, 17th to 18th century hipped roof building of three storeys, with a timber-framed 16th century hall house wing on its north-east corner. The east side of the main house has a late 18th century semi-octagonal bay with an open arcaded ground floor.

Hughenden Manor was a medieval manor owned by the Dormer family of Wing after 1538. During the 18th century, the existing farmhouse was extended into a 13 bay brick house and, in 1862, Benjamin Disraeli commissioned Lamb to make alterations, adding brick facings and pseudo-Jacobean details.

ST. MARY'S CHURCH, GREAT MISSENDEN

Manor Farm is a fine 18th century house in chequered brick and other buildings worth seeing are 18th century Church Farm, 19th century Pigott's, which was the home of Eric Gill, the graphic artist and painter, Brands House in Kingshill Road, an early 18th century stuccoed house and Grange Farm at Widmer End, a late medieval house with cruck trusses.

LITTLE MISSENDEN CHURCH

LITTLE MISSENDEN COTTAGES

THE LEE;
CHOLESBURY; CHARTRIDGE;
ASHLEY GREEN

The Liberty family (of Regent Street) bought the Manor House at *The Lee* in 1900 and created the picturesque green at the centre of the village, adding houses and improving cottages around it.

The old church is largely of the 13th century with lancets, piscina and sedile. Fine wall-paintings include a 15th century St Christopher and there is a 14th century foliate decoration and a 13th century consecration cross. The church-yard memorial to the Liberty family is an Art Nouveau celtic cross.

Cholesbury is scattered along the Hawridge to Buckland Common Road.

St Laurence Church has a 13th century nave and 14th century chancel. The pre-1710 wooden bell-turret has a saddleback roof. The church sits within Cholesbury Camp, a well-preserved Iron Age fort.

Cholesbury Windmill was rebuilt as a tower mill, using the existing cap-fantail and machinery of the earlier smock mill and is now a dwelling.

Chartridge is made up of a scattering of hamlets and farms to the west of Chesham, but the village street itself stretches for a mile to the north west of the town. Asheridge Farm is a brick-encased 15th century timber-framed hall house. Limetree Farmhouse (17th century) has a brick front dated 1729, and Old Zac's and Raymond's Cottage make up an early 17th century timber-framed house with jettied cross-wing.

Old Oak Farm at *Ashley Green* has a fine group of 17th century farmbuildings. Grove Farm is part of a 13th century manor house with 15th century windows and, nearby, fragments of a gatehouse stand within a partially water-filled inner moat, which in turn is surrounded by an outer moat.

VILLAGE GREEN, THE LEE

CHESHAM

Situated on the River Chess, the town based itself on the mills which existed in the Middle Ages and was granted a market in 1257. Lace-making, straw-plaiting and chair-bodging became important during the 18th century but in the 19th century, factory-based industry, like boot and shoe manufacture, took over.

The town stretches along the valley and converges on the market place. The river threads its way through the southern part of the town, its bridges and banks creating an appealing environment amongst the older houses and streets.

The church of St Mary stands in Lowndes Park, which itself is divided from the town centre by St Mary's Way. It is a large, heavily restored, flint building with a 12th century window, 13th century arcades and some 15th century stained glass.

There are some attractive 18th and 19th century houses in Church Street, often with facades screening earlier timber-framed structures. The Bury is a grand 18th century house built about 1712 by William Lowndes of Winslow Hall. Other noteworthy buildings in Church Street include Lantern House, numbers 114-116 and the Queen's Head pub of 1830.

New Footpath has a terrace of Victorian cottages, flint-faced and laced with red brick.

In Fuller's Hill stands Germains, with its timber-framed medieval wing and handsome 18th century addition. Little Germains dates from 1540, with a 1720 L-shaped addition to the road. The High Street with its Market Square must originally have been similar in character to Old Amersham but the 18th century Market Hall was demolished in 1965. A recent neo-Classical Clock Tower is now the street's only landmark.

THE OLD SCHOOL HOUSE, CHESHAM

BURY LANE COTTAGES, CHESHAM

AMERSHAM

The old town of *Amersham* lies in the Misbourne Valley on the ancient route through the Wendover Gap in the Chilterns. The Metropolitan Railway Station was sited on the hill above the old town in 1892 and nearly all subsequent development took place around it, creating two very distinct and separate entities. This has been a rich blessing, as it is the best preserved old town in the county and is a fascinating architectural showcase along the whole length of its High Street.

The church of St Mary, a large medieval flint building, was heavily restored during the 19th century. The Drake Chapel has some interesting family monuments dating from 1623 onwards. The distinctive Market Hall, which is still in use, stands in the centre of the High Street and was built in 1682 by Sir William Drake of Shardeloes.

Heddons House has a 16th century jettied range to the street and Apsley House, with its late 17th century front, is set back from the pavement and has bay windows and a Classical pilastered doorcase with a roundel. The Gables is early 17th century with shaped gables and two canted bay windows with mullioned and transomed windows. Red Lion House is a late 17th century timber-framed house.

The King's Arms is a picturesque inn with an original 16th century hall and cross wing. The eastern part is a very convincing imitation Tudor extension of 1936. Elmodesham House, the town's largest house, was built in 1720 and added to in 1900. Of purple and red brick, it has two and a half storeys and is eleven bays wide.

Sir William Drake's Almshouses of 1657 are single storey buildings grouped around three sides of a forecourt, with gabled wings to the High Street. Miss Day's Almshouses of 1875 form a charming Classical brick terrace.

On the western outskirts of Old Amersham, on a commanding hilltop site, stands Shardeloes, the home of the Drake family. Built between 1758 and 1767 by Stiff Leadbetter, the house was altered and completed by Robert Adam, who took over in 1761.

THE MARKET HOUSE, OLD AMERSHAM

At the top of the hill between old and new Amersham, stands High and Over, a seminal modern house in the Le Corbusier mould, designed in 1929-30 by Amyas Connell for Professor Ashmole of London University, its white, rendered brick walls and horizontal windows contrasting sharply with the woodland greenery of the steep site. It has a hexagonal core and three radial wings with canopied roof terraces. Four years after this, Connell designed the Sun Houses, just down the hill in Highover Park. Built this time entirely of in situ concrete, they also have strip windows, glazed staircase walls and roof canopies. The courage and boldness of both clients and architect are impressive.

92

THE KINGS ARMS, AMERSHAM

HIGH AND OVER, AMERSHAM

HIGH WYCOMBE;
WEST WYCOMBE

The town sits in a valley in the Chilterns, flanked by hills. The centre is small and predominantly of the 18th century but the town, as a whole, is sprawling and featureless. The parish church and castle mound was established by the 11th century. The wide High Street was probably laid out during the 12th century as part of the Oxford to London route and the medieval market place stretched from the Guildhall to the top of Frogmoor.

During the 18th century, *High Wycombe* was the most prosperous market town in Buckinghamshire, and fine houses were built along Frogmoor, the High Street and Easton Street. The Guildhall and the Shambles were also built at this time. Predominant industries were lacemaking, paper-making and chair-making. The railway arrived in 1847 and the furniture industry thrived from then on. During the 20th century the M40 and M25 motorways brought the town into the orbit of the Thames Valley and its culture of high technology industries.

All Saints Church has 13th century remnants but is mainly Perpendicular and has a tower dating from 1535.

The Guildhall of 1757 stands in Cornmarket and was designed by Henry Keene. It partially closes the western end of the High Street and is of red brick with stone dressings over an open arcaded cornmarket. Each front has a projecting pedimented centre. The stone arcading is Tuscan and the whole building shows strong Palladian influences. The Little Market House was designed by Robert Adam in 1761 to rehouse the Shambles and the Buttermarket.

In the High Street, there are many elegant 18th century fronts on both sides, including The Falcon Hotel and the Midland Bank.

Situated on the extreme western outskirts of High Wycombe, *West Wycombe* village manages to retain an identity of its own, with its main street of picturesque 16th to 17th century timber-framed cottages, some of which hide behind 18th and 19th century stucco or brick facades.

On the hill above the village stands the spectacular medieval church of St Lawrence, remodelled in the Palladian style in the mid-18th century, with its tall tower and prominent crowning golden ball. The Dashwood family mausoleum of 1765 also stands on the same hill, a hexagonal form with a parapet of urns.

Prominent buildings in the High Street include Church Loft, a late 15th century timber-framed house, with a queenpost roof and oversailing upper floor at front and rear and a carriageway. The Steps, a five bay Georgian house, The George and Dragon, an early Georgian inn and the former White Hart Inn, a 16th to 17th century timber-framed house with jettied upper floor, are also outstanding.

West Wycombe Park is the creation of both the first and second Sir Francis Dashwood between 1707 and 1771. The principal architect was Morise Lewes Jolivet, a pupil of Servandoni, with later additions by Revett although much of the work appears to have been carried out by draughtsman John Donowell up to 1760. The house stands in a beautiful park on the River Wye, which was widened and dammed to create a lake in the shape of a swan, and is one of the county's finest buildings. It is long and irregular with several different facade treatments and the tour de force is the south front. The eleven bay facade has a two-storey Palladian colonnade, with free-standing stuccoed brick ground floor columns and stuccoed timber first floor columns with a pediment over the three central bays. Very attractive verandahs are thus formed at both levels, providing shade to the walls of adjoining rooms. The Main Hall has a red Wilderness and Portland stone floor with a brick hypercaust beneath. Other notable features of the house include the Ionic west portico based on the Temple of Bacchus at Teos, the Temple of Apollo, and the Tuscan east portico which is based on the Villa Rotunda at Vicenza. The park is adorned with temples, pavilions and water features.

THE GUILDHALL, HIGH WYCOMBE

WEST WYCOMBE PARK

WEST WYCOMBE VILLAGE STREET ▷

IBSTONE; TURVILLE; FINGEST; SKIRMETT; LANE END; CADMORE END; WHEELER END

Ibstone church has Norman south and north doorways, a 13th century chancel with lancet and a weatherboarded bell-turret.

Cobstone windmill is a smock-mill of 1830 with twelve sides and three storeys, four sails and a fan tail.

Turville and Turville Heath are situated in a beautiful part of the Chilterns, locked into a network of narrow, meandering lanes along the Oxfordshire border. The landscape is an undulating patchwork of woodlands and heaths and has an intimate scale unmatched elsewhere in the county.

St Mary's Church is medieval, with a Norman north doorway, 13th century tower and chancel arches and a 16th century crown-post roof. There is stained glass by John Piper made by Patrick Reyntiens in 1975.

Fingest nestles on the valley floor, enclosed by rising fields and woodlands on three sides and opens out to the south in the direction of neighbouring Skirmett.

At the heart of the village stands the imposing church of St Bartholomew, its twin saddleback roof crowning a Norman tower. At the bell stage on each side are large two-light openings, double-shafted with roll-mouldings in the arches. The north doorway dates from 1200 and the chancel is of the 13th century with lancets.

The small hamlet of *Skirmett* is situated in a delightful pastoral valley between Fingest and Hambleden and has a number of timber-framed houses, including Crooked Chimney Cottage (16th century), with exposed cruck trusses in the gables, Old Crown House and Isabel Cottage, dated 1618.

At *Cadmore End* the brick and tile kiln of 1830 is square, with a shallow dome and a central round chimney.

FINGEST CHURCH

Houses and farmhouses are scattered around a broad common at *Wheeler End*. Chipp's Manor of 1733 is built of vitreous brick with red brick dressings over five bays and two storeys, with a parapet crowned by urns.

HAMBLEDON MANOR

FAWLEY; HAMBLEDEN; MEDMENHAM; HARLEYFORD MANOR

St Mary's Church, *Fawley*, has a 13th century tower, with a Perpendicular top stage and the nave dates back to the 12th century. In the vestry is a Tree of Life in stained glass by John Piper and Patrick Reyntiens, made in 1977.

Fawley Court is situated two miles away from the village on the banks of the Thames and was begun in 1684. The gardens are laid out in formal terraces and, during the 1770s, Capability Brown worked here. The Gothic ruin of 1732 and the Fishing Temple by Wyatt of 1771 on Temple Island in the middle of the Thames are two of the main features designed for the house.

Hambleden is a pretty village with a large green or common on the north side of the churchyard, extending into seductively beautiful countryside. Cottages of brick and flint form a broken edge to this green and, to the east side, stands the Manor House, built in 1603 and thereafter much altered. The pubs, the post office and cottages cluster against the south side of the churchyard .

St Mary's Church was originally a Norman cruciform building, but the central tower was removed and replaced in 1720 by a brick west tower. 13th and 14th century details abound but restorations in 1859 have given the building a distinctly Victorian feel.

Medmenham Abbey was a Cistercian house founded early in the 13th century, but the present building is partly of 1569, partly 18th century Gothic and mostly designed in 1898 by Romaine-Walker. Danesfield House (1899 to 1901), also by Romaine-Walker, was built in Tudor style in white chalk with red tiled roofs and clustered brick chimneys. The house stands partially within Danesfield Iron Age Hill-fort, with its southern defence to the Thames.

Harleyford Manor was built in 1755 for Sir William Clayton and designed by Sir Robert Taylor. Of five-by-five bays and of red brick in Rococo and neo-Classical style, it is an idiosyncratic building standing on a superb site on the banks of the Thames.

MARLOW; LITTLE MARLOW

In the early 18th century, *Marlow* was a convenient loading place for barges transporting goods by the Thames to London. However, it was already popular as a riverside resort and grew in prosperity when a number of fine houses, such as Marlow Place and Court Garden, were built. The wooden bridge was eventually replaced in 1829-31 by the suspension bridge we see today. Designed by William Tierney Clark, a pupil of Telford, its chains are anchored to two brick arches faced with Bath stone and carried on piers.

All Saints Church of 1834 stands prominently at the north end of the bridge.

The river frontage is quite rural in character with trees and low buildings set in gardens. The town quickly peters out to the west as the Thames curves seductively away towards Henley. The former Town Hall is on the Market square and was designed by Samuel Wyatt in 1806-7 . In the High Street, number 41 is a five-bay, three storey, mid-18th century vitreous brick house with red brick dressings. The George and Dragon is also 18th century, of red brick, with a three-bay central pediment. Marlow Place was designed by Thomas Archer in 1720 for the 1st Earl of Portsmouth.

Other notable buildings in the town include Marlow Ferry (1700), Malt House (18th century). Thames Lawn (18th century), Old Bridge House (1860), Brampton House (Georgian), the Whitbread Brewery (18th century), Lloyd's Bank (1900) and the Old House in West Street.

The earliest parts of *Little Marlow* church are of the 12th century and the arcades are 14th and 15th century.

The late 16th century timber-framed Manor House had a 19th century range added with a hipped roof. The staircase is 17th century with an arcaded balustrade.

Other buildings to see in the area are Fern House, a former workhouse and lace factory of 1780. Westhorpe House off Marlow Road, (18th century), and Monkton Farmhouse, about a mile to the north. The Abbey, about one mile to the east, is the remains of a Benedictine nunnery founded before 1218.

MARLOW SUSPENSION BRIDGE

BEACONSFIELD; PENN; COLESHILL

Like Amersham, *Beaconsfield* falls into two distinct and separate parts, the original town with its coaching inns and the new town, with suburbs close to the railway station.

The old town is grouped around a crossroads and composed of four ends, London, Wycombe, Aylesbury and Windsor and lined with 15th, 16th and 17th century houses, often disguised by 18th century brick facades.

The Old Rectory is a 16th century house (1534) of two storeys around three sides of a courtyard, enclosed on the fourth side by a high wall of pink brick with diaper patterning, in which there is a central stone arched entrance. The upper floor and the walls to the courtyard are timber-framed, whilst the gable ends of the wings are jettied out over the brickwork and have ogee-curved bracing.

In Wycombe End, in a side passage to the churchyard, stands Capel House of 1524. It was built as the church house and is of Wealden-type construction, with curved braces in the central recessed section.

London End has the finest collection of buildings, starting with the Saracen's Head, a 16th century inn. Several brick-fronted timber-framed houses on the north side include Essex House, Highway House, and The Malt House. The former Bull Farm and Bull Inn is a complex that stretches from number 49 to number 55 and has timber-framed wings and hay barns of the 16th and 17th centuries. Wilton Park Farm is an 18th century farmhouse with a timber-framed granary on straddle stones, a stable and a barn.

The former Crown Inn has a stuccoed front with five canted bays with pretty octagonal 18th century glazing bars and an arched carriageway entrance. Behind the frontage it has a 15th century timber structure with a wing at right-angles to the street and a 16th century hall range attached at the street end.

Sandwiched between High Wycombe and Beaconsfield, Penn is hardly a distinct village now, but has a fine 14th to 15th century church,

THE OLD RECTORY, BEACONSFIELD

with a queenpost nave roof resting on stone figures and heads and a timbered porch doorway with tracery.

There are many pre-1650 timber-framed cottages at *Coleshill* including Red Lion Cottages (1620) and part of Forge House (15th century).

CAPEL HOUSE, BEACONSFIELD

CHENIES; THE CHALFONTS; LATIMER; JORDANS; GERRARDS CROSS

The model village of *Chenies* is set amongst the beeches above the Chess Valley. It was named after the Cheynes who acquired the manor in the 13th century, but the manor house was owned by the Russells (the Dukes of Bedford) from 1525 until 1957.

The Manor is built close to the church in mellow brickwork and has a 15th century west wing, a south wing dated 1525 and was remodelled by Blore in 1829. The undercroft, which stands apart, is of the 13th to 14th centuries.

St Michael's Church was rebuilt in the 15th century and restored in the late 19th century.

The Bedford Chapel was added in 1556 and has impressive monuments to several members of the Russell family, including John, the first Earl, who died in 1555.

Chalfont St Giles church is of flint and has a 13th century chancel, a 14th century south aisle and a Perpendicular clerestory and tower. There is an important cycle of wall-paintings of 1330 in the south aisle.

Milton's Cottage is of the early 17th century, a timber-framed and brick infilled house, in which the poet John Milton lived from 1665 to 1674.

The church tower at *Chalfont St Peter* fell down in 1708 and the church was rebuilt in 1714.

In Denham Lane stands Mopes Farm, a 16th century timber-framed building and two 18th century weatherboarded barns.

At Shrub's Wood is an International Modern house designed by Mendelsohn and Chermayeff in 1933. Set amongst the trees of an old estate, this is a fine example of modern architecture built in monolithic reinforced concrete and plastered white.

St Mary Magdalene Church, *Latimer*, was designed by Edward Blore in 1841 and rebuilt by G G Scott in 1867.

Latimer House (1832-38) was designed by Blore for Lord Chesham in Tudor style, in red brick with stone dressings. Picturesque timber-framed village cottages dating from the 16th and 17th centuries cluster around the Green.

FRIENDS' MEETING HOUSE, JORDANS

The village of *Jordans* is a model settlement of 1919 created by Fred Rowntree for the Quakers. Jordans Village Industries was established to secure an economic base for the community, but lasted only until 1923.

The Friends' Meeting House in Welders Lane was built in 1688 by Isaac Penington and is set in a lush wooded valley. The brick house has plain walls, a hipped roof and a coved eaves cornice. Old Jordan's Farm is of the 17th century and, before the Meeting House was built, was used as such. The barn is timber-framed and weatherboarded and is said to incorporate timbers from the Mayflower.

On West Common at *Gerrards Cross*, facing the heath and duckpond, are several fine Georgian houses. Walpole House is 17th century with a plain 18th century brick front. Latchmoor is a 19th century villa and Latchmoor House, of the same period. has a Doric portico. Camp Road skirts the site of an Iron Age hill-fort with a double rampart.

MILTON'S COTTAGE, CHALFONT ST GILES

IVER; IVER HEATH; WEXHAM; HEDGERLEY

St Peter's Church, *Iver*, has some Anglo-Saxon stonework, a 12th century north aisle, a tower with lancets, 13th century south aisle and chancel and late Perpendicular windows and clerestory.

Iver Grove in Wood Lane was built for Lady Mohun between 1722 and 1724 and is one of the finest Baroque houses in the county. Of two storeys, it is five bays by three. On the west front there is a three-bay pediment on giant Doric pilasters with matching cornice and frieze. The house could be the work of John James and shows the influence of Wren, Hawksmoor and Vanbrugh. It has a comfortable domestic scale and sits well in its unpretentious garden. Pinewood Film Studios of 1935 are situated at Iver Heath, just to the north of Iver.

St Mary's Church, *Wexham*, is largely of flint, has a Norman nave and chancel and a circular west window. The weatherboarded bell-turret has a spire.

Langley Park is a much altered mid-18th century house designed by Leadbetter as a hunting lodge. The former British Cement Association buildings and landscaped areas in the grounds of Wexham Springs House, are an interesting relic of concrete design and technology between 1947 and 1967.

Known as a source of bricks in the 18th and 19th centuries, *Hedgerley* also attracted potters. Roman pottery kilns have been discovered nearby.

St Mary's Church was built by Ferrey in 1852.

Other noteworthy buildings are Old Keepers Cottage, Dean Cottages, Metcalfe Farm, The White Horse (all 17th and 18th century), Old School Cottage (1844), The Old Rectory (18th century), the Old Quaker House (16th century) and Shell House, a chequer brick building of 1680.

IVER GROVE

FARNHAM; STOKE POGES; WOOBURN

St Mary's church, *Farnham Royal*, has a medieval chancel and some 12th to 13th century details but was mostly rebuilt after 1868.

Stoke Poges village is dispersed. The medieval church and the 16th century manor house of the Hastings family stand on the edge of Stoke Park, the late 18th century creation of John Penn, grandson of William Penn, who named Pennsylvania in the USA.

St Giles Church is a picturesque site seen from Stoke Park and through the lychgate one sees the three gables of the 1558 brick built Hastings chapel, the chancel and the nave. A large tiled roof sweeps down over nave and aisles. The Norman core was added to during the 13th century, when lancets, a piscina and the tower were built. The timber porch is Decorated with open sides of ogee lights and quatrefoils in the spandrels.

The Gray Monument was designed by Wyatt in 1799 and erected outside the churchyard, as a memorial to the poet Thomas Gray and to his 'Elegy in a Country Churchyard'.

Stoke Park is a Georgian mansion built for John Penn in 1789, by Nasmith and Wyatt. Wyatt added four corner pavilions linked by colonnades and the dome was built as a belvedere.

Other buildings worthy of note are The Clock House, 1765 almshouses by Thomas Penn, the Vicarage (1802-4), a castellated brick house by Wyatt and Stoke Place (1698) with wings of 1750-70 by Leadbetter and grounds laid out by Capability Brown.

St Paul's Church in Town Lane, *Wooburn*, has medieval origins but was almost entirely rebuilt in the 1860s. There are good 15th and 16th century brasses.

Old Vicarage has a 15th century cross-wing and some contemporary wall-painting on the ground floor. Boscobel House and Barn are mid to late 16th century with timber-framing, brick infilling, and weatherboarding.

STOKE POGES CHURCH

THE TORTOISE FOUNTAIN, CLIVEDEN

CLIVEDEN; DROPMORE

The previous house at *Cliveden* for the Duke of Buckingham by Winde and built between 1664 and 1677, was remodelled by Thomas Archer in 1705. In 1795 the house was burnt down and the rebuilt house again burnt out in 1849, leaving only Archer's pavilions and Winde's terrace, which acts as a plinth for the present house.

This house was designed by Sir Charles Barry and completed in 1851. Reminiscent of the Villa Albani in Italy, it has a nine-bay front and two and a half storeys. The ground floor is rusticated and there are giant Ionic pilasters above ground floor.

The entrance porte-cochere by Clutton is on the north front. There are single storey wings to pavilions and a bold top balustrade with vases. The Clock Tower of 1861 is also by Clutton. Fine internal features of the house include the 16th century stone fireplace in the hall, the French Rococo panelling in the Dining Room and a Jacobean overmantel and panelling in Nancy Astor's former bedroom. The house stands on a magnificent elevated site overlooking the Thames and the park contains specially themed gardens lavished with sculpture. South of the house is a broad plateau of lawns, with a parterre close to the Terrace and, at the southern extremity, an enclosing raised circle of turf called 'The Ring'. Features of the park include the Tortoise Fountain, the Octagon Temple of 1735, the Fountain of Love, the Blenheim Pavilion and the Queen Anne Vase of 1725.

Down by the Thames are several lodges and cottages designed by Devey after 1869.

Dropmore House was begun in 1792 for Lord Grenville, King George III's Prime Minister, with the south range designed by Samuel Wyatt in Neo-Classical style. The gardens are laid out with walkways, a grotto and an Italian Garden with a loggia and central fountain.

DORNEY COURT

◁ *CLIVEDEN*

BURNHAM; TAPLOW; DORNEY; BOVENEY

There are substantial survivals of monastic buildings at *Burnham* Abbey which was founded as a house of Augustinian canonesses in 1266. After the Dissolution, it became a ruin by 1787 but was restored at the outbreak of World War 1. The east range of the Cloister exists, as do the 13th century Chapter House doorway, the Warming House and the Parlour.

The Tithebarn is aisled with arched braces and queen-strut trusses and the Dovecote is a thatched 16th century structure.

Hunterscombe Manor has a 14th century hall with a timber-framed core.

The medieval village of *Taplow* stood close to the Thames next to the famous Saxon burial ground but a new church was built further east, around which grew a cluster of Victorian and Edwardian houses, which now form the centre of the village.

Maidenhead Railway Bridge was designed by Brunel in 1838 and is the bridge made famous in JMW Turner's painting, 'Rain, Steam and Speed'.

St James Church, *Dorney*, and Dorney Court stand together on the flat meadows of the Thames reaches. The church nave originates from the 12th century, has 13th century windows and a 14th century porch. The 17th century Garrard Chapel is built of brick.

Dorney Court is an enchanting late Tudor house, which has been in the Palmer family since 1530. It is of timber-frame construction with mellow pink brick nogging and has a clay tile roof with many gables. The earliest parts are the atmospheric 15th century Great Hall and the contemporary Parlour Wing at the eastern end, with its 1740 staircase. Remarkable features of the Parlour are the two polygonal bays added in the 16th century, and the fireplace is late 15th century. The house is beautifully furnished with solid oak and lacquered pieces and with centuries of family portraits.

The isolated chapel of St Mary Magdalen on the banks of the Thames at *Boveney*, is built of chalk rubble, has a Norman west window and Norman north and south doorways. The bell-turret is weatherboarded.

DORNEY COURT

BIBLIOGRAPHY

The Buildings of England: Buckinghamshire Nikolaus Pevsner and Elizabeth Williamson

A History of Buckinghamshire Michael Reed

Chilterns Scene Chris Andrews

The Chilterns Hepple and Doggett

The English Heartland Robert and Monica Beckinsale

Changes in our Landscape Eric Meadows

The Illustrated History of the Countryside Oliver Rackham

TINKERS END COTTAGE, OVING

PLACES OPEN TO THE PUBLIC

NT: National Trust   NGS: National Gardens Scheme

Stowe, Nr Buckingham	NT	NGS	Chequers, Nr Ellesborough		
Waddesdon	NT	NGS	Hampden House, Great Hampden		
Dorney Court, Dorney			Nether Winchendon House, Lower Winchendon		NGS
Ascott House, Wing		NGS	Shardeloes, Amersham		
Cliveden	NT	NGS	Hughendon, Nr Hazlemere		NGS
Gayhurst, Nr Newport Pagnell			Chenies Manor, Chenies		
Tyringham House, Nr Newport Pagnell		NGS	Milton's Cottage, Chalfont St. Giles		
Chicheley Hall, Nr Newport Pagnell			Fawley Court, Medmenham		
Claydon House, Middle Claydon	NT		West Wycombe House and Park, West Wycombe	NT	NGS
Wotton House, Wotton Underwood			Hedgerley Nature Reserve, Hedgerley		
Bletchley Park, Bletchley, Milton Keynes			Friends' Meeting House, Jordans		
Linford Manor, Great Linford, Milton Keynes			Model Village, Beaconsfield		
Winslow Hall, Winslow		NGS	Pinewood Film Studios, Iver Heath		
Wolverton Rural Industries Museum, Wolverton, Milton Keynes			Turville Park, Turville		
Pitstone Mill, Pitstone, Nr Ivinghoe			Dropmore House, Dropmore		
Liscombe Park, Soulbury			Tythrop House, Kingsey		NGS
Mentmore House, Mentmore			Hartwell House and Gardens, Hartwell		
Dorton House, Dorton			Biddlesden Park, Biddlesden		
Notley Abbey, Long Crendon			Great Linford Wildfowl Centre, Milton Keynes		
Boarstall Tower, Boarstall			The Cowper and Newton Museum, Olney		

INDEX

*Numbers in **bold** indicate illustrations*

THORNBOROUGH MANOR, THORNBOROUGH

Books Published by
THE BOOK CASTLE

JOURNEYS INTO BEDFORDSHIRE: Anthony Mackay *(Pocket format)*
Foreword by The Marquess of Tavistock, Woburn Abbey.
A lavish book of over 150 evocative ink drawings.

HISTORIC FIGURES IN THE BUCKINGHAMSHIRE LANDSCAPE: John Houghton
Major personalities and events that have shaped the county's past, including a special section on Bletchley Park.

TWICE UPON A TIME: John Houghton
Short stories loosely based on fact, set in the North Bucks area.

MANORS and MAYHEM, PAUPERS and PARSONS: Tales from Four Shires:
Beds, Bucks, Herts and Northants: John Houghton
Little-known historical snippets and stories.

MYTHS and WITCHES, PEOPLE and POLITICS: Tales from Four Shires:
Beds, Bucks, Herts and Northants: John Houghton
Anthology of strange but true historical events.

BUCKINGHAMSHIRE MURDERS: Len Woodley
Nearly two centuries of nasty crimes.

LEAFING THROUGH LITERATURE: Writers' Lives in Hertfordshire and Bedfordshire:
David Carroll
Illustrated short biographies of many famous authors and their connections with these counties.

BETWEEN THE HILLS: The Story of Lilley, a Chiltern Village: Roy Pinnock
A priceless piece of our heritage – the rural beauty remains but the customs and way of life described here have largely disappeared.

A PILGRIMAGE IN HERTFORDSHIRE: H. M. Alderman
Classic, between-the-wars tour round the county, embellished with line drawings.

THE HILL OF THE MARTYR: An Architectural History of St. Albans Abbey:
Eileen Roberts
Scholarly and readable chronological narrative history of Hertfordshire and Bedfordshire's famous cathedral. Fully illustrated with photographs and plans.

JOHN BUNYAN: His Life and Times: Vivienne Evans
Highly-praised and readable account.

SUGAR MICE AND STICKLEBACKS: Childhood Memories of a Hertfordshire Lad:
Harry Edwards
Vivid evocation of those gentler pre-war days in an archetypal village, Hertingfordbury.

KENILWORTH SUNSET?: A Luton Town Supporter's Journal: Tim Kingston
Frank and funny account of football's ups and downs.

A HATTER GOES MAD!: Kristina Howells
Luton Town Footballers, officials and supporters talk to a female fan.

THE STOPSLEY BOOK: James Dyer
Definitive, detailed account of this historic area of Luton. 150 rare photographs.

PUB WALKS FROM COUNTRY STATIONS: Buckinghamshire and Oxfordshire:
Clive Higgs

PUB WALKS FROM COUNTRY STATIONS: Bedfordshire and Hertfordshire:
Clive Higgs
Two books, each of fourteen circular country rambles, starting and finishing at a railway station and incorporating a pub-stop at a mid-way point.

FAMILY WALKS: Chilterns North: Nick Moon
Thirty shorter circular walks.

FAMILY WALKS: Chilterns South: Nick Moon
Thirty 3 to 5 mile circular walks.

CHILTERN WALKS: Hertfordshire, Bedfordshire and North Buckinghamshire:
Nick Moon

CHILTERN WALKS: Buckinghamshire: Nick Moon

CHILTERN WALKS: Oxfordshire and West Buckinghamshire: Nick Moon
A trilogy of circular walks, in association with the Chiltern Society. Each volume contains 30 circular walks.

COUNTRYSIDE CYCLING IN BEDFORDSHIRE, BUCKINGHAMSHIRE AND HERTFORDSHIRE: Mick Payne
Twenty rides on- and off-road for all the family.

Further titles are both published and in preparation. Available via any bookshop.
Full details from:
THE BOOK CASTLE
12 Church Street, Dunstable, Bedfordshire LU5 4RU.
Telephone: 01582 605670